FREEFORM

STUDENTS' BOOK 2

MICHAEL DOWNIE
DAVID GRAY
JUAN MANUEL JIMÉNEZ

Richmond ENGLISH

THE SANTILLANA PUBLISHING GROUP

Richmond English
19 Berghem Mews
Blythe Road
London W14 OHN

Richmond English is part of the Santillana Group

© Santillana, S.A. 1993
© Michael Downie, David Gray &
Juan Manuel Jiménez 1993
First published 1993

ISBN: 84-294-3689-8

Depósito legal: NA 13 11 1993
Printed in Spain by: Gráficas Estella, S. A.

Authors' acknowledgements

The authors would like to thank the editorial team
for their hard work and enthusiastic support on the
project. Thanks also to our colleagues for their help
and advice. Finally, thanks to our families for their
patience and encouragement throughout.

Publisher's acknowledgements

Design
Giles Davies

Cover
Giles Davies

Picture research
Sandie Huskinson-Rolfe (PHOTOSEEKERS)

The publishers would like to thank the following
for permission to reproduce their material.

Photographs
Adidas (UK) Ltd., page 26; Allsport (UK) Ltd., page 19B, 19C
(photo Tony Duffy); Apple Computers (UK) Ltd., page 82;
Barnabys Picture Library, pages 77 *above left*, 85 *above right*;
John Birdsall, pages 17 *left*, 17 *right*, 77*above right*, 77 *below left*;
The Boots Company PLC, page 27 *centre right*; Britstock-
IFA/NASA/Eric Back, page 85 *centre right*; Canon (UK) Ltd.,
page 26; The J. Allan Cash Photolibrary, page 67A, 67C, 67D;
Colorific, page 35; Chris Fairclough Colour Library, pages 67B,
95B; J.Hosking/FLPA, page 40; Fortean Picture Library, page
61; The Francis Frith Collection, pages 84 *below*, 85E; Hulton-
Deutsch Collection Ltd., pages 19A, 85 *above centre*, 85G; The
Image Bank, page 77 *below right*; The Kobal Collection, page
89; The Mansell Collection, page 85D; National Railway
Museum, York, page 85F; Panasonic Consumer Electronics
UK, page 27 *centre left*; Philips Consumer Electronics, page 27
above right; Jenny Acheson/Retna, page 84 *above*,
Photofest/Retna, page 31 *above*, Philip Saltonstall/Onyx/Retna,
page 19D, Timothy White/Onyx/Retna, page 30C; Rex
Features Ltd., pages 7B, 7D, 13, 17 *centre left*, 30D; Sony (UK)
Ltd., pages 26, 27 *below*; Spectrum/NASA, page 85 *above left*;
Frank Spooner Pictures Ltd., page 30B; Sporting Pictures (UK)
Ltd., pages 7C, 21 *below*, 51; Tony Stone Images, pages 17
centre right, 92A, 92B, 92C, 95A; Sygma, pages 28, 30A, Mauro
Carraro/Sygma, page 12, T. Orban/Sygma, page 7E, Jeffrey
Markowitz/Sygma, page 7A; Syndication International, page 31
below; Telegraph Colour Library, page 18; Topham Picture
Source, page 21 *above*; Vaughn/Becker/ZEFA, page 53 *centre*.

All remaining commissioned photographs by Gareth Boden
with art direction by Sandie Huskinson-Rolfe
(PHOTOSEEKERS).

We are grateful to everyone who helped with the location
photography, especially the following people:
Mrs Ashbys shoe stall and Harlow market; Balfour News,
Bishops Stortford; British Rail, Bishops Stortford; Burnt Mill
School, Harlow; Gluttons Cafe, Bishops Stortford; Harlow
Traffic Police, Essex; Hertfordshire Constabulary at Bishops
Stortford; Herts and Essex Hospital, Bishops Stortford; Juicy
Duck, Bishops Stortford; The Spiritual Warriors.

Illustrations
Kathy Baxendale, page 99, *The Guardians* title, all handwriting;
Jerry Collins, page 59 *bottom*; Giles Davies, page 43;
Stephen Dew, pages 57 *left*, 73, 83 *right*; Andy Hammond,
pages 39, 52 *bottom left*, 67 *top*; Louise Hill, pages 66 *top*, 94, 98
Jane Hughes, pages 118, 120 *left*; Ann Johns, pages 44 *bottom
left*, 57 *right*, 61, 66 *bottom*, 68, 80, 97, 105 *right*, 110 *bottom left*;
Frances Lloyd, pages 8 *top right*, 9, 11, 52 *top left*, 65, 67 *bottom*,
74, 83 *left*, 86, 100, 105, 112 *left*, 115, 120 *right*;
Doreen McGuinness, page 117; Ed McLachlan, pages 8 *bottom
right*, 40, 76, 91 *bottom left*, 106, 112 *right*; Steve Noon, pages
23, 37, 55, 69, 87, 101; Mark Payne, pages 14, 15, 88, 90, 103 *left*,
110 *top left*; Adrian Salmon, page 70; Michael Salter, page 50;
David Simmonds, pages 75, 110 *right*; Peter Utton, pages 34,
71, 79, 91 *top left and bottom right*; Lis Watkins, pages 12, 16,
25, 44 *top right*; Gary Wing, pages 38, 41, 47; Madeline Winter,
page 60.

CONTENTS MAP

A new start

1 WESTGATE KIDS
EPISODE 1

1 Match the phrases to a scene.
Where's he from?
He's really unfriendly.
Who's he?
Yeah, see you.
He's a singer.

1 It's Alejandro Sanz.

2 He's Spanish. He's gorgeous.

3 Look, there's Mike.
So what?

4 Can I help you?
Yeah, I want to order *Smash Hits*.

5 OK, I need to fill in a form.

6 Hi, Dave.
Hi, Mike.
See you later.

7 Do you like him?
Yeah, he's all right. Why?
I don't.

2 [cassette icon] **Listen to check.**

3 Listen again. Copy and complete the order form.

ORDER FORM
66

Name: ...Michael...

Age: ....

Address: ....North...........

....

....

Phone number: ....

Occupation: ....

>>> 1 p121

2 Language study
Personal information

RECORD CARD

First name: Susan
Surname: Dale
Age: 15
Address: 28 Trent Road
Phone number: 987 1144
Nationality: English

1 Write the six questions Susan answered for her record card.
Example:
What's your first name?

2 Interview your partner using the questions and make a record card for him/her.

3 Pairwork Famous people

1 Match the famous people to their occupations.
politician
singer
basketball player
actress
model

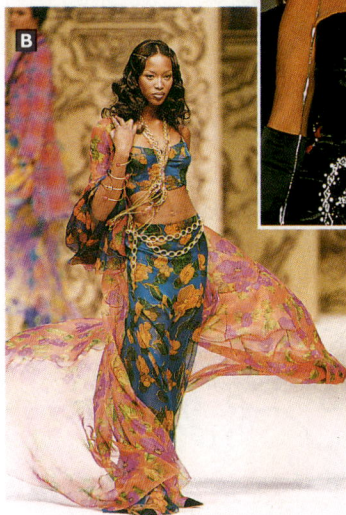

2 Make a record card for each person.

3 Turn to PAIRWORK A1 p102 to check.

4 Role play Party talk

1 Unjumble the speech bubbles to find the dialogue.

Grandet.

Are you English?

What's your first name?

Paris.

Hello.

Oh, how do you spell that?

See you later.

How old are you?

Yes, I am.

Hi.

G..R..A..N..D..E..T.

No, I'm not. I'm French.

What's your surname?

Fifteen.

OK, bye.

Are you a student?

Ann.

Where are you from?

2 PAIRWORK. Choose a role.

A Turn to PAIRWORK A2 p102
B Turn to PAIRWORK B1 p109

5 Tune in Class project

Listen to these teenagers. Copy and complete the table showing their likes (✔) and dislikes (✗).

	Simon	Jeremy	Helen	Ann
reading				
comics				
discos				
going to the cinema				
school				

2 p121

6 Language study

Talking about likes and dislikes

1 **Listen again. Copy and complete these sentences with *do*, *does*, *don't* or *doesn't*.**

1 ____ you like going to the cinema?
Yes, I ____.
2 ____ Jeremy like school? No, he ____.
3 ____ you like discos? No, I ____.
4 ____ Ann like reading comics?
Yes, she ____.

2 **Write sentences about the teenagers. Start like this:**
Simon likes/does not like...

7 Find out

1 Write down five things you like doing.
Example:
I like watching TV.

2 Interview two other students to find two things you all like doing.

8 Pairwork Good friends

A Turn to PAIRWORK A3 p102
B Turn to PAIRWORK B2 p109

9 Sounds right

· **1 Copy the grid. Write a different letter of the alphabet in each square.**

2 Listen to your teacher and cross the letters you hear.

3 Shout *Bingo* if you cross all the letters.

4 Play the game in groups of four.

10 Spot check

1 Ask questions to find out whether your partner likes doing these things.
Example:
Do you like eating hot dogs?
– Yes, I do. / No, I don't.

- eating hot dogs
- listening to music
- learning English
- drinking Cola
- going to the cinema
- reading newspapers
- going to concerts

2 Write sentences about your partner.
Example:
My partner doesn't like listening to music, but he/she likes eating hot dogs.

Trends

1 READING *Survey*

1 Look at the survey questions. Which questions are missing?

2 Are these statements true or false?

1 83 girls like watching television in their free time.

2 63 boys like reading comics.

3 40 girls but only 37 boys like reading science fiction stories.

4 57 boys like watching music programmes.

3 Add four more statements and ask your partner to check them.

4 How old do you think the people in the survey are?

Survey questions

In our national youth club survey we asked teenagers four questions.

1 Do you like watching TV?

2...

3...

4...

Our results show the differences in taste between boys and girls of the same age.

Results: free time

	Girls	Boys
Watching television	49	69
Reading books	36	35
Going out with friends	125	126
Listening to music	70	90

Results: reading

Girls =
Boys =

100
75
50
25
0

63 · 36 · 57 · 85 · 45 · 40

Comics · Adventure stories · Science fiction stories

Results: television

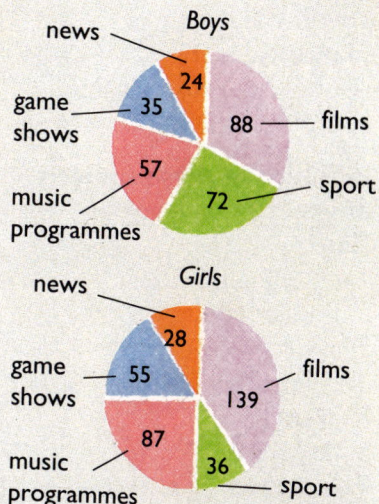

Boys
news — 24
game shows — 35
films — 88
music programmes — 57
sport — 72

Girls
news — 28
game shows — 55
films — 139
music programmes — 87
sport — 36

2 LISTENING *Numbers*

Listen to the results of the survey. Copy and complete the table.

type of film	boys	girls
adventure		
terror		
comedy		
science fiction		
cowboy		
romance		

3 VOCABULARY *Word fields*

1 Match these words to a word spider.

visiting family   going to the countryside   soap operas
documentaries   playing tennis   cartoons

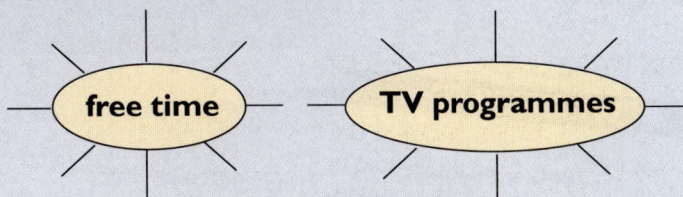

free time   TV programmes

2 Add one more idea to each spider.

4 FOLLOW UP *A survey report*

1 Choose one of the survey questions and interview three students in your class.

2 Present your information like this:

Name: .... Date: ....

Topic: ....

Number of students interviewed: ....

Summary: ....

UNIT 2 Top 40

1 In print

1 Look at the magazine cover. What type of magazine is it?
sports car music fashion computer gossip

2 Which of these subjects appear in this issue of *Zap*?

1 cinema and films
2 music
3 sport
4 computers
5 animals
6 fashion
7 cars
8 horoscopes
9 travel

3 Which title on the magazine cover refers to this article?

Zap!
OCTOBER ISSUE

90p

This week's competition win a mini hi-fi

Van Damme tells Zap! about his new film

FREE! Giant poster of your favourite band *See page 16*

Top 40 run down PLUS!
WRITE TO A STAR
Centre pages
HOROSCOPES
VIDEO GAMES
PHOTO STORY
POP GOSSIP

HOT SOUNDS Best CDs of the month

From Schoolroom to Stardom
3 teenagers who want to be megastars talk about their lifestyles

3 brilliant posters!!!
Van Damme
Kylie Minogue
Donnie Wahlberg

Fashion How to look great at the weekend

Special Feature Teenage trends Are you a typical teenager?

● MUSIC

Our *Zap!* survey shows that the majority of teenagers are very interested in music. They have a favourite band or singer, and usually buy a record, cassette or CD once a month. The average teenager is big business for the music industry. We went into the streets to find out what you spend your money on. Here are some typical comments:

● **Lynne** (15), *from Hull* - I listen to a lot of music. My favourite group is NKOTB. I always buy a music magazine at the weekend. I like reading about new bands.

● **Patrick** (14), *from Liverpool* - I never buy records - I buy CDs. They are expensive, but the quality is fantastic.

● **Susan** (15), *from London* - Records, cassettes, CDs and music magazines. Oh, and I sometimes go to a pop concert on Saturday.

● **Kevin** (16), *from Lichfield* - I always buy Zap! You are brilliant! I collect all your issues.

4 Listen. Which teenager is being interviewed?

»» 3 p121

5 Complete the sentences with *in the morning, on Saturday, during the week*.
1 I listen to the radio when I get up ____.
2 ____ I listen to music on my way to school.
3 ____ I sometimes go to a concert.

2 Language study

Adverbs of frequency

1 Copy and complete the graph with these words.

sometimes   usually   often

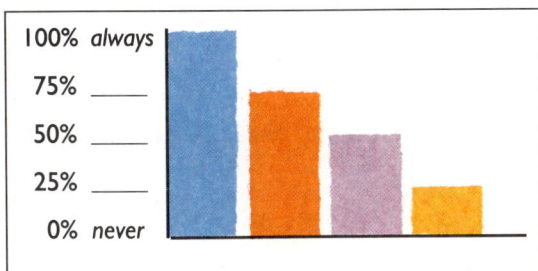

2 Complete the questions.

Example:

listen to/music/morning?

Do you listen to music in the morning?

1 listen to/music/evening?
2 watch/music programmes/evening?
3 buy/music magazines/Saturday?
4 go to concerts/weekend?
5 go to discos/week?

3 Interview your partner using the questions.

Example:

Do you listen to music in the morning?
– Yes, always.

4 Write a report using your partner's answers.

Example:

My partner always listens to music in the morning.

3 A day in the life of

1 Read this article from the magazine and answer the questions.

1 Why is Graham a typical teenager?
2 Why is he different from other teenagers?

Graham is a typical teenager. He gets up early to go to school. He always studies in the afternoon and watches television in the evening. He usually goes to bed at 10.30. But he is typical with a difference - hundreds of other teenagers ask him for his autograph.

He is lead singer in a young Manchester band called *Road to Nowhere*. We asked him to tell us more about the band.

'I go to a local secondary school during the week and I usually practise with the band on Friday evening. There are four of us in the band. We love playing music and singing. We are not professionals, but people think our music is good. We are quite famous in our area. We sometimes give a concert on Saturday at a disco or youth club, it depends. When we don't, we like visiting music shops and buying CDs or records. I often buy a music magazine to find out what new bands are doing.'

2 Write the questions the interviewer asked Graham.

Example:

What time do you get up?
When do you practise with the band?

3 Work in pairs. Act out the interview.

4 Tune in Top ten

1 [cassette icon] **Listen to three teenagers talking about music.**

1 Which song do they all like?

2 Which song do they all dislike?

ALL TIME FAVOURITES

TOP TEN

1	Madonna *Holiday*	**6**	Prince *Purple Rain*
2	Guns and Roses *Sweet Child of Mine*	**7**	Michael Jackson *Billy Jean*
3	Rolling Stones *(Can't get no) Satisfaction*	**8**	Police *Roxanne*
4	Soft Cell *Tainted Love*	**9**	Queen *Bohemian Rhapsody*
5	Dire Straits *Romeo and Juliet*	**10**	Led Zeppelin *Stairway to Heaven*

2 Listen again. Which of the expressions do you hear?

- He's great.
- I think it's boring.
- It's really fantastic.
- It's not bad.
- I think he's terrible.
- I really hate it.
- She's OK.
- It's my favourite.
- I think he's brilliant.
- I don't know.

 >>> 4 p121

5 Language study

Giving opinions

1 Match the expressions from Activity 4 to a face.
Example:

A   B   C

He's great.

2 Find out what your partner thinks of the singers or bands in the top ten list.
Example:
What do you think of Madonna?

6 Pairwork The interview

[icon] **A** Turn to PAIRWORK A4 p103
[icon] **B** Turn to PAIRWORK B3 p109

7 Opinions

1 Unjumble the speech bubbles to find the dialogue.

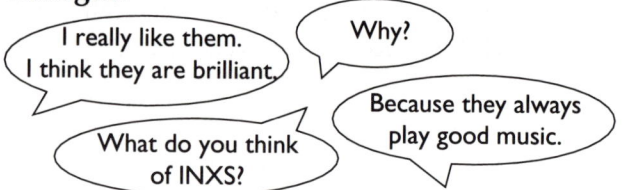

I really like them. I think they are brilliant.

Why?

Because they always play good music.

What do you think of INXS?

2 Write the names of three bands or singers you like.

3 Find out what three other students think about them.

8 Star spot

1 Complete the personal profile with these words.

height   and   likes   has   thinks   fantastic

Name: Chesney Hawkes
Born: 1971
1 _____: 1.70 m
First hit: 'The One and Only'.
Sold over 100,000 copies.
Number one for five weeks.
Facts: He 2 _____ three dogs, one cat, a rabbit, one brother 3 _____ a sister.
Gossip: He thinks Pete Townsend is 4 _____ and he really 5 _____ Madonna. He 6 _____ racism is terrible and racists are boring!

2 Write a personal profile for your favourite pop star.

9 Dictation

1 Write the name of a pop star or band.
Example: *Vanilla Ice*

2 Dictate the letters to your partner jumbled up.
Example: N A L A V L I   C E I

3 Unjumble the letters your partner dictates to you.

10 Spot check

1 Choose a title.
My teacher   My mum/dad   My best friend

2 Write a paragraph about the person.
Include the following information: *name, age, height, likes, dislikes.*

WRITING *Fan club mail*

1 Look back at the magazine cover. Where can you find this information in the magazine?

Zap! FAN CLUBS

Where to contact your favourite star!

● **MADONNA**
PO Box 1400
New York
NY 10020 USA

● **MARTIKA**
947 Fairway Drive
Walnut
California
CA 91789 USA

● **JASON DONOVAN**
PO Box 292
Watford
Herts WD2 4ND GB

2 Complete the fan letter with these words.

usually   seeing   favourite
at the weekend   fantastic

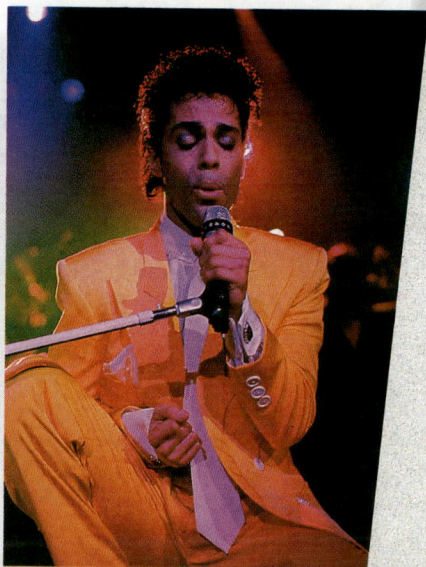

> Dear Prince,
> I am sixteen years old and I come from Manchester. Your music is
> 1 _____ and I really want to join your fan club.
> I 2 _____ listen to your music at my friend's house - she has a CD player.
> 3 _____ I often go to discos or parties and I always ask the DJ to play your records. My 4 _____ song is Purple Rain.
> Why don't you come to Manchester again? You're great on TV, but I love 5 _____ you on stage.
> Please, please send me a signed photo and tell me how to join your fan club.
> Love,
> Annabel

3 Do you like Prince? Why/Why not?

4 Choose a different pop star. Write a fan letter to him/her.

Undercover

1 Private detective

1 Look at the cartoon. What mistake does Magnut make in his first important case?
1 He follows the wrong person all day.
2 He arrests the wrong person at the airport.

2 Complete the sentences with these words.
buying   into   going   thin   leaving
black hair   coming

3 🎧 **Listen to check.**

4 Which of these sentences describe what is happening in the last scene?
1 Lola is smiling.
2 The nun is talking to Magnut.
3 Magnut is arresting Lola.
4 Magnut is laughing.
5 The dog is biting the nun.
6 Lola is wearing a yellow hat.

5 p121

2 Language study

Present continuous

1 Match these expressions to an appropriate sentence.

usually   at the moment

1 Magnut tries to find lost cats and dogs.
2 Magnut is following Lola.
3 Lola stays in five-star hotels.
4 Lola is staying in a hotel on First Avenue.

2 Complete what Lola says with the correct form of the verbs in brackets.

I (1 come) from Australia. I (2 be) a diamond smuggler. I always (3 travel) by plane. I (4 fly) to Paris today. I (5 sit) in a comfortable chair and I (6 drink) a glass of champagne. I (7 celebrate) my escape from Magnut.

3 Work in pairs. How many different questions can you write about the text in one minute?

Example:

Where is Lola from? Is she from Australia?
Where is she flying? Is she flying to London?

3 Game Cards

1 Work in groups.

2 Look at the illustrations and choose one. Write what Magnut is doing on a paper square and put the square in a box.

3 One person chooses a square from the box and mimes the activity.

4 The first person to guess what Magnut is doing has the next turn.

Example:

I think Magnut is laughing.
– Yes, he is. / No, he isn't.

4 Pairwork Silent movies

Write the story of Magnut and Lola.

A Turn to PAIRWORK A5 p103
B Turn to PAIRWORK B4 p110

5 Tune in Police file

📻 **Listen to the radio announcement and choose the correct picture from the police file.**

a
Age: 25
Height: 1.55 m
Weight: 70 kg

b
Age: 25
Height: 1.80 m
Weight: 90 kg

c
Age: 25
Height: 1.80 m
Weight: 95 kg

>>> 6 p121

6 Language study
Describing people

1 Copy and complete these descriptions with *is* or *has got*.

> He 1_____ 25 years old. He 2_____ tall and muscular. He 3_____ a square face. He 4_____ blue eyes and a long thin nose. He 5_____ short blond straight hair.

> He 1_____ 25 years old. He 2_____ short and thin. He 3_____ a thin face and blue eyes. He 4_____ long dark hair and a moustache.

2 Match the descriptions to the two other illustrations on the police file.

3 Match the phrases to the correct boxes.

She is ...	She has got ...

tall   green eyes   thin   16 years old
black hair   a long nose

4 When do we use *to be* and when do we use *have got* to describe a person's appearance?

7 Game Who is it?

1 Work in pairs. Choose a face. Your partner asks questions to find out which face you chose.
Example:
Has she got a round face?
– Yes, she has. / No, she hasn't.

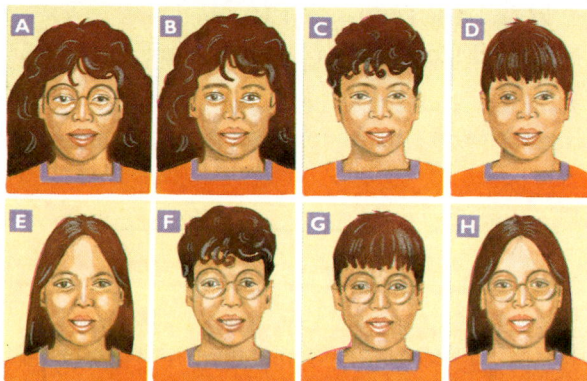

2 The person who asks the least number of questions wins.

8 Pairwork Spot the difference

🧑‍🤝‍🧑 **A** Turn to PAIRWORK A6 p103
B Turn to PAIRWORK B5 p110

9 Sounds right Contractions

1 When we speak, we normally use the contracted form of *to be* and *have got*.
Example:
I'm from London. / She's got a brother.

2 📻 Listen to these sentences.
1 I have got brown eyes.
2 I am listening to music.
3 She is my sister.
4 My parents are not at home.
5 They are at my Gran's house.

3 Listen again and repeat.

4 Listen to the next five sentences. How many words are there in each sentence?

10 Spot check

1 Write six sentences describing a pop star or a television personality. Do not write his/her name.
Example:
X has got brown hair. / X is short.

2 Read your sentences to your partner. Can he/she guess who you are describing?

Lifestyles

Punk

Heavy Metal

1 READING *Fashions*

1 Work in pairs. Do you like the different fashions in the photographs?

Rap

New Romantic

2 Read the letter from a British girl to her pen-friend.

3 Find the clothes words in the letter and make a list.

I don't really have time to try different fashions. We wear a uniform for school – very boring! In the winter it's a dark blue skirt and jumper with dark shoes and a coat. In the summer it's a light dress and a blazer.

At weekends I usually go out with my friends. We all like wearing jeans and trainers. When we go to parties I wear my brother's big blue denim jacket and there's always my favourite red shirt for special occasions. I love it and my friends think it's great!

2 LISTENING *Time*

1 ☐ Listen to a teenager talking about a typical Saturday. Copy and complete the table with the times mentioned.

get up	
meet friends	
go to a friend's house	
get home	
go to a disco	
get home	

2 Ask your partner questions to find out what time he/she does things on Saturday.
Example:
What time do you get up on Saturday?

3 VOCABULARY *Word order*

1 Look at the table. Copy it and add some more words of your own.

	1 size	2 shape	3 colour	4 material	noun
1	big	——	blue	denim	jacket
2	——	——	green	——	eyes
3					
4					
5					
6					

2 Now make five sentences using the information in the table.
Example:
I usually wear a big blue denim jacket.

3 Write two sentences about the clothes your partner is wearing.

4 FOLLOW UP

1 Work in groups. Choose one of these places.
• a disco • a party • school • a friend's house

2 Design clothes for a boy and a girl in this place.

3 Tell the class about your designs.
Example:
Our boy and girl are at a disco.
He's wearing ... / She's wearing ...

Sport

1 The history of the Olympic Games

1 Look at the Olympic flag. What do the circles represent?

THE OLYMPIC GAMES became famous in the Greek world in the sixth century BC. Every four years athletes travelled many miles to take part in them. The ceremony was originally a religious festival in honour of Zeus. However, in 394 AD, the Roman emperor Theodosius I decided to stop the festival, so there were no Games for more than 1000 years.

A Frenchman, Baron Pierre de Coubertin, convinced thirteen nations to take part in the first modern Games in Athens in 1896.

The Olympic Games still take place every four years and the event is very important for sportsmen and women all over the world. Sometimes there are problems. In 1916, 1940 and 1944 the Olympic Games did not take place because of war. In 1980, the US team did not go to the Moscow Games and in 1984 the team from the USSR did not go to the Games in Los Angeles.

Luckily, when people remember the Olympic Games of the past they remember the good parts: the gold medals, the new world records and, of course, the mascots. Perhaps the most popular mascot in modern times was Cobi, the friendly dog who introduced the 1992 Olympic Games in Barcelona. ❏

2 Read the text and complete the table.

Modern Olympics	
Place	Date
Athens	1896
Moscow	
Los Angeles	
Barcelona	

3 📼 Listen to a person talking about the history of the Olympic Games. How many mistakes does he make?

⟩⟩⟩ **7** p121

2 Language study

Simple past: *be*

1 How many past tense forms of the verb *be* can you find in the text?

2 Which form is singular and which is plural?

3 Complete the paragraph with *was* or *were*.

1992 1____ a great year for Spain. There 2____ the EXPO in Seville, Madrid 3____ the cultural capital of Europe, and of course, there 4____ the Olympic Games in Barcelona. The Games 5____ a great success. A total of 183 countries 6____ there and 1,691 sportsmen and women won medals. There 7____ also 750,000 spectators and the Spanish royal family 8____ there. In fact, it 9____ the King who declared the Games officially open.

3 Words...words...words

1 Match the sports to where they are played.
Example: squash - *court*
squash motor racing basketball badminton athletics hockey rugby golf horse racing

pitch course track court

2 Look at the vocabulary cards. Copy and complete the last two.

Sport: *karate*
Useful verbs: *practise, kick*
Place: *gym*
Equipment: *mat, belt*

Sport: *tennis*
Useful verbs: *play, serve, return*
Place:
Equipment:

Sport: *football*
Useful verbs:
Place:
Equipment:

3 Make a vocabulary card for one more sport.

4 Compare your cards with your partner's.

4 Gold medalists

1 Choose two photographs and write sentences about them.
Example:
Jesse Owens was an athlete at the 1936 Olympic Games in Berlin. He was the winner of four gold medals.

a Jesse Owens/athlete 1936/Berlin/4 medals

b Torvill and Dean/ice-skaters 1984/Los Angeles/1 medal

c Mark Spitz/swimmer 1972/Munich/7 medals

d Janet Evans/swimmer 1988/Seoul/3 medals

2 Ask your partner about the photographs he/she chose.
Example:
Who was Jesse Owens?
Why was Jesse Owens famous in 1936?

3 Think of another Olympic gold medalist. Tell your partner about him/her.
Example:
Arancha Sanchez was a tennis player at the 1992 Olympic Games in Barcelona. She was the winner of two medals. One was silver and one was bronze.

5 Tune in A sports quiz

1 Match the answers to the questions.
1 Who did the Dream Team play in the final of the Barcelona Olympics?
a) Germany   b) Croatia   c) Great Britain
2 When did the Winter Olympics start?
a) 1930   b) 1900   c) 1924
3 Which city held the Olympics in 1908 and 1948?
a) New York   b) London   c) Madrid
4 When did the Olympic flag first appear?
a) 1914   b) 1896   c) 1931
5 How many athletes competed in the Barcelona Games in 1992?
a) 4,000   b) 12,000   c) 10,000

2 🔲 **Listen. How many questions does the contestant answer correctly?**

➤➤ 8 p121

6 Language study
Simple past: regular/irregular verbs

1 Study this:

compete	win
compet**ed**	**won**
did not compete	**did not** win
Did you compete?	**Did you** win?

2 Do the same for these verbs.
play go run watch
swim join do see

3 Complete the questions and interview your partner.
Example: play football / last week?
Did you play football last week?
– Yes, I did. | No, I didn't.
1 play football/last night?
2 run to school/two days ago?
3 swim in the sea/last summer?
4 join a sports club/last year?
5 do any sport/last week?
6 watch sport on television/last weekend?

4 Write sentences about your partner.
Example:
My partner did not play football last night.

7 Do you know?

1 Answer the questions in pairs.
1 How many medals did Spain win in the last Olympics?
2 Which team won the last World Cup?
3 Who was the winner of the Tour de France last year?

2 Write three questions of your own to ask another pair.

8 Pairwork A sporting accident!

A Turn to PAIRWORK A7 p103
B Turn to PAIRWORK B6 p110

9 Dictation Simple past

1 Match the verbs to the correct pronunciation of the -ed ending.
liked   /ɪd/
wanted   /d/
arrived   /t/

2 Make a list of six regular verbs in the simple past.

3 Read your list to your partner.

4 Write the verbs in the correct column.

/t/	/d/	/ɪd/

10 Spot check

1 Make a list of ten verbs you think are useful.

2 Write the past tense of each verb.

3 Compare them with your partner's.

WRITING *Biographies*

1 Look at the photograph of Clare Francis. What type of sport does she do? Why do you think she is famous?

2 Read the questions.
1 Where was Clare Francis born?
2 What did she study at university?
3 Why did she leave marketing?
4 What did she do in 1973?
5 Who did she marry?
6 What did she write for television?

3 Read the text and answer the questions.

4 Complete the text with these words.
but   at   and   when   in
about   in   across

5 Use the information about Miguel Indurain to write a paragraph.

Clare Francis

Clare Francis was born in Surrey 1_____ 1946. She studied Economics 2_____ University College, London. 3_____ she finished, she began a career in marketing, 4_____ became bored with city life. She really loved sailing and when she inherited some money she decided to buy her own boat. In 1973, Clare sailed 5_____ the Atlantic single-handed. 6_____ 1977, she married a Frenchman 7_____ they had one son. In the following years she became one of Britain's most popular sportswomen. She won many yachting races and wrote a television series 8_____ ships and sailing.

Miguel Indurain / born / Villava, Navarra / 1964. He / study /the local school / until / he / be /eighteen.
1982 / he / finish / his studies/ and / he / become / professional cyclist.
Then / he / join / the Banesto team.
He / win / the Tour de France / 1991 and 1992.
1992 / he / also / win /the Giro d'Italia.

6 Choose a sports personality. Write a paragraph about him/her. Include a drawing or photograph.

Review and Extension 1

1 Grammar

■ Present simple

1 Write ten sentences about a person in your family, five true and five false. Include information about his/her:

age
physical description
likes/dislikes
routine

Example:
My sister is twelve. She has got brown eyes.

2 Read the sentences to your partner.

3 Guess which of your partner's sentences are true and which are false.

4 Ask your partner five more questions about people in his/her family.

■ Present continuous

1 Write what you think five famous people are doing at the moment.

Example:
The King is eating breakfast.

2 Work in groups. Mime each of your sentences to the group. Can they guess who the person is and what he/she is doing?

■ Simple past

1 Write six questions to ask your partner about last weekend.

Example:
What time did you get up?

2 In pairs, ask and answer the questions.

3 Which pair in the class can talk for the longest about last weekend?

4 Choose another topic to talk about.

last Monday   last night   last lesson

2 Vocabulary

1 Work in pairs. You have three minutes to add as many words as possible to the word spiders.

leisure activities

nationalities

2 Compare your work with that of another pair. Did you think of the same words?

3 In conversation

1 Work in pairs. Say these expressions in your language.

1. How do you spell her surname?
2. Do you like her?
3. What's she wearing?
4. What does she usually do at the weekend?
5. What type of music do you like?
6. What do you think of disco music?
7. I think it's quite good.
8. Were you at home last night?
9. What did you do?
10. See you later.

2 You are at a disco with your best friend. Use five of these expressions in a dialogue.

3 Act out your dialogue for another pair.

4 Study skills Dictionaries

1 Label the dictionary definition.
a **Headword**: the word you look up.
b **Phonemic transcript**: the sound of the word you look up.
c **Part of speech**: tells you that the word is a noun, a verb, etc.
d **First sense**: the first meaning of the word in the dictionary.
e **Second sense**: the second meaning of the word in the dictionary.

> **table** /teibl/ **1** N A table is a piece of furniture. It has legs and a smooth, flat top. **2** N A list of facts or numbers set out in columns on a piece of paper.

2 How many people in your class have got dictionaries? Do they bring them to school? Are they bilingual or monolingual dictionaries? What size are they? Write a report.

The Guardians

News in brief

STORMS EXPECTED
Bad weather will arrive off the coast of Santa Marta today. Winds will reach speeds of over 150 kilometres per hour and rain will keep visibility to a minimum. There will be violent storms at sea.

1 The adventure diary

1 Look at the picture and answer the questions.
1 Where are the teenagers?
2 What are they doing?

2 Write a name and a personality for each teenager. Include:
Name
Age
Likes / Dislikes

3 Choose one of the teenagers to be your character.

4 Ask other students about their characters to find your perfect partner.

You are now in your adventure teams. Good luck!

2 Voices

Listen. Which words do you hear?
storm   hurricane   wind   cold   snow
strong winds   waves   hot

3 Investigate *The climate*

Turn to Investigation file 1 p115

23

A new friend

1 WESTGATE KIDS
EPISODE 2

1 Unjumble the scenes of the story.

1
You dropped this.
Wow, it's Matt!
Oh, thanks.

2
What about these? They're our most popular brand.
How much are they?

3
Do you go to Westgate School?
Yeah.

4
Careful! Why don't you watch where you're going!
It's Mike. Typical!
Sorry.

5
Here you are.
Have you got anything brighter?

6
Can I help you?
Yes, I'm looking for a pair of trainers.

7
£20
I was there last year.
My purse!

8
I know.

9
What about going for a drink?
Yeah. OK.

2 Listen to check.

9 p121

24

2 Language study Suggestions

1 Match the parts of the sentences.

| Why don't we
What about | going to the cinema?
the cinema?
go to the cinema? |

2 Write suggestions for each of these situations.

1 Friday night with your family.
2 Three friends visit your house on Saturday.

Example:

Why don't we go to the cinema?

3 Role play Cheaper, please!

1 Work in pairs. Unjumble the speech bubbles to find the dialogue.

How much are they?

Yes, I'm looking for a pair of jeans.

Black, please.

Can I help you?

Here we are.

£40.

Have you got a cheaper pair?

Yes, that's great.

What colour do you want?

What about these? They're only £25.

2 Where does the dialogue take place?

3 Choose a different type of shop and write your own dialogue. Act it out.

4 Pairwork A perfect present

1 Match each present to the appropriate person.

A £15
B £35
C £125
D £55
E £45
F £28
G £30
H £50

Barry really likes outdoor sports. He spends his free time playing team games with friends.

Julie loves going to discos and dancing. She is a real music fanatic. She also really likes going to concerts.

Terry likes adventure sports. He likes taking risks and he goes to the countryside every weekend to climb or canoe down a river.

2 Work in pairs. Write the names of three students in your class. You have £160 to spend on presents. Decide which presents to buy them.

Example:

A: *Mary likes sport. Why don't we buy her a tennis racket?*

B: *Yeah, OK. And what about a pair of trainers?*

A: *No, she's got a new pair of trainers.*

5 Tune in Brand names

1 Look at these brand names. What products do you associate with them?

adidas **SONY**
Canon **Wrangler**

2 Add two more brand names and a product for each one.

3 ▣ **Two teenagers are discussing the advantages and disadvantages of buying a well-known brand. What things do they mention?**

1 last longer   5 better design
2 more reliable   6 more expensive
3 cheaper   7 more fashionable
4 more colourful   8 less popular

4 Do you agree with them?

»»» 10 p121

---

6 Language study

Comparatives and superlatives

1 Copy and complete the ad for a new pocket calculator with these adjectives.

larger   attractive   best   easier   great
effective   smallest   low   quicker

> **COMPUTECH**
> Are you looking for a more 1_____ way to work with numbers? COMPUTECH is 2_____ than other models and has a 3_____ memory. It is one of the 4_____ pocket calculators you can buy, so it is 5_____ to carry than other models. It combines the most 6_____ design with 7_____ cost. For the 8_____ results and 9_____ value buy COMPUTECH!

2 Complete the table with the appropriate forms of the adjectives.

adjective	comparative	superlative
		smallest
		best
	quicker	
	larger	
		most attractive
	easier	

3 Find two more adjectives from the Westgate kids, Episode 2 to add to the table.

---

7 Favourite things

1 Write what your favourite possession is on a piece of paper.

2 Work in pairs. Compare your favourite things with these words. How many of the words can you use?

useful   useless   attractive   expensive   cheap   interesting   boring   old   good   bad
Example:
My skateboard is cheaper than your bicycle.
– Yes, but my bicycle is more useful.

8 Game Compare it

1 Work in groups. Write these words and add four of your own to the list.
computer   television   pen   football

2 In turns, choose a word and say an adjective you associate with it.
Example: *television - expensive*

3 Look at the list of adjectives you have made for each object. In turns, write a sentence comparing the objects.
Example:
A television is more expensive than a pen!
A television is the most expensive.

4 The person who thinks of the most sentences wins.

9 Sounds right

1 ▣ **Listen to this sound.** /ə/

2 Listen and repeat these words.
faster   slower   better   computer   America

3 Copy these sentences and underline the sound /ə/.
1 A computer is faster than a typewriter.
2 My brother is taller than my sister.
3 America is larger than Spain.
4 A camera is more expensive than a calculator.

10 Spot check

1 Find an example of adjectives which:
1 end in *-er* and *-est* in the comparative and superlative.
2 end in *-ier* and *-iest* in the comparative and superlative.
3 use *more* and *most*.

2 Can you find any irregular forms?

ASSIGNMENT 3

Products

1 READING *Features*

1 Read and answer the questions.

1 How many of these personal stereos have a radio?

2 What features does the Philips have?

3 Which personal stereo has the most features?

2 Which personal stereo do you think is the most expensive/the cheapest?

3 Compare them using these words.

colourful   complicated   good   attractive   comfortable

Example:

The Panasonic is more attractive than the Philips.

2 LISTENING *Prices*

1 Copy the list of personal stereos.

1 BOOTS   2 PANASONIC

3 PHILIPS

2 Listen and write the prices of each one.

3 VOCABULARY *Labelling*

Label the pictures with these words.

a cassette player   a radio

a music system   a CD

A

B

C

D

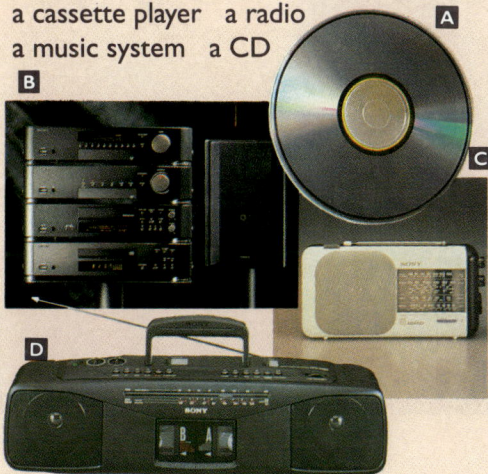

PERSONAL STEREOS UNDER £50

PHILIPS MOVING SOUND AQ6404

Features: Rewind, Fast Forward, Auto-reverse, no radio.

Is it any good? Not bad! Very good bass sound. Interesting blue colour!

Rating ★★

PANASONIC RQ535V

Features: All the things the others have, plus lots of interesting extras like a 3-band Equaliser, Dolby and a good radio.

Is it any good? It has a brilliant sound.

Rating ★★★★★

BOOTS 'WICKED' PSX20

Features: Rewind, Fast Forward, anti-rolling mechanism, stereo headphones, no radio.

Is it any good? Yes! Great sound and very trendy appearance.

Rating ★★★

4 FOLLOW UP *Brand name survey*

1 Find out what brand of trainers people wear.

2 Ask questions to complete the table with the ratings information.

Example:

How much do your trainers cost?

How comfortable are they?

What do you think of the design?

Ratings

★★★★★ Brilliant

★★★★ Very good

★★★ Good

★★ OK

★ Poor

Make	Price	Comfort	Design
Reebok	★★	★★★★	★★★
Adidas			
Nike			
Ellesse			

3 Which is the most popular brand of trainers? Why?

4 Make a similar table for brands of jeans. Which is the most popular brand? Why?

Movie mania

1 Star watch

1 Write down any information you know about Kevin Costner. Read the text quickly to check.

2 What information about him is included in the text?
Personal details
Political opinions
Likes/Dislikes
Career history
Family life
Achievements

3 Find words in the text which mean the same as:
1 how directors choose actors/actresses for a part in a film
2 very important
3 to play a part in a film (or a play)
4 a famous actor/actress
5 an American award for actors/actresses
6 capacity to do something

4 📼 Listen to a Kevin Costner fan. Why does the fan admire him?
1 for his role in *Robin Hood*
2 because he is handsome
3 because he has got a lot of personality
4 for his acting abilities

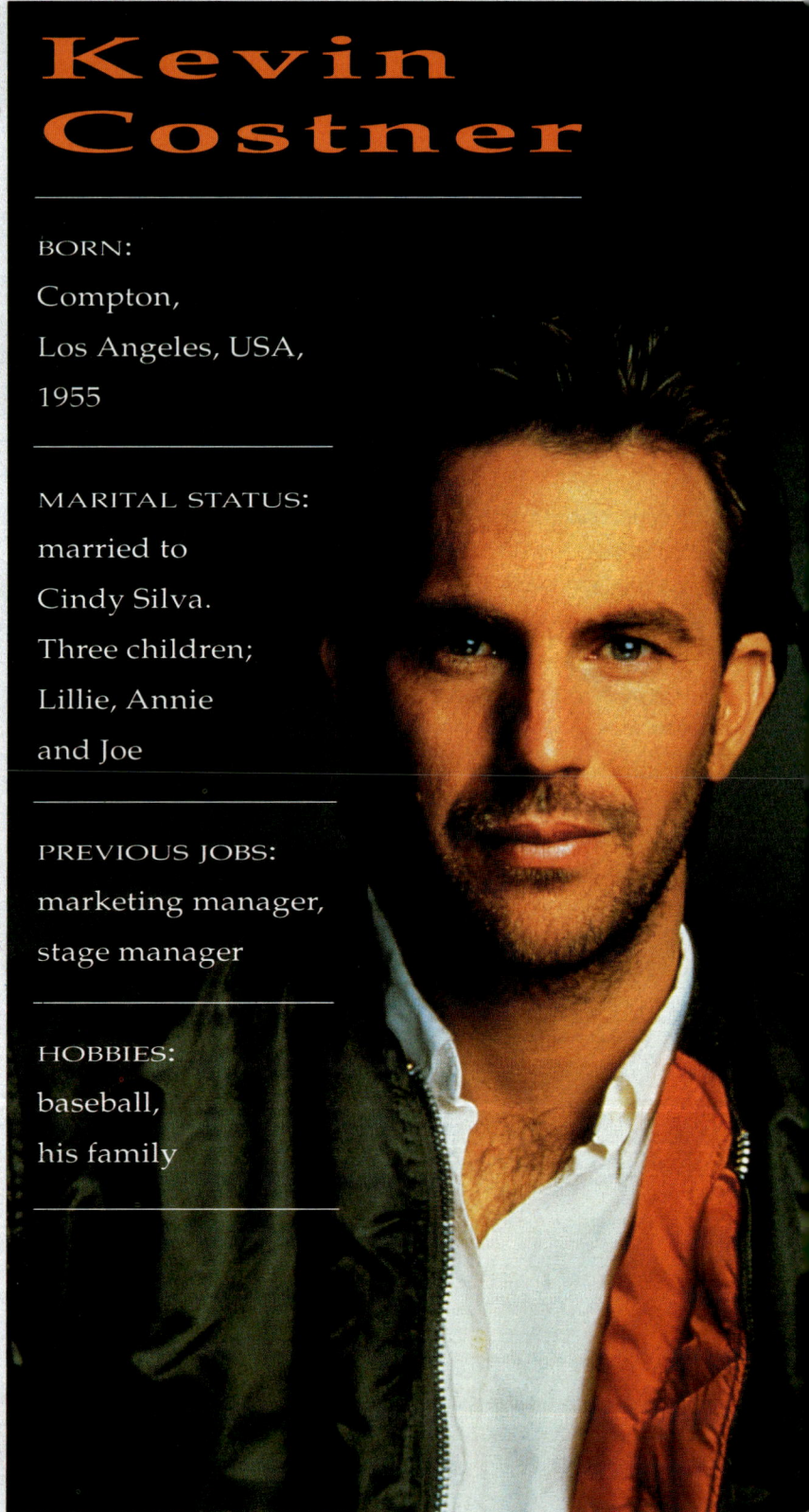

PROFILE

Kevin Costner

BORN:
Compton,
Los Angeles, USA,
1955

MARITAL STATUS:
married to
Cindy Silva.
Three children;
Lillie, Annie
and Joe

PREVIOUS JOBS:
marketing manager,
stage manager

HOBBIES:
baseball,
his family

BACKGROUND

Born in Los Angeles, Kevin first started acting at college (Berkeley). When he left college he became a marketing manager, but after a month he was bored. He decided to leave and went to Hollywood where his film career began. He worked as a stage manager, but went to hundreds of auditions. His first major role was in *Fandango*, a film inspired by Spielberg. The following year he acted in *Silverado* which led to *The Untouchables* with Sean Connery. Suddenly, Kevin Costner was a star. In 1991, he won an Oscar for his performance in *Dances with Wolves*. His acting abilities in this film were at their best. Kevin is a very friendly person. He really enjoys the outdoor life and he also likes listening to Madonna's music.

THE MOVIES

1987	The Untouchables
1987	No Way Out
1989	Bull Durham
1989	Field of Dreams
1990	Revenge
1991	Dances with Wolves
1991	Robin Hood: Prince of Thieves
1992	JFK
1993	The Bodyguard

2 Language study
Short answers

1 Match the answers to the questions.
1 Do you like Kevin Costner? Yes, he has.
2 Are you a fan of his? No, he can't.
3 Did you see his last film? Yes, I do.
4 Can he sing well? No, I didn't.
5 Has he got any children? Yes, I am.

2 Look at the questions and answers. Which verb is used in each of the short answers?

3 Find someone who ...

Work in groups. Find someone in your group who ...
... has got two brothers.
... likes football.
... went to the cinema last week.
... can sing well.
... thinks Kevin Costner is a good actor.

4 Role play Stars

1 In pairs, choose a film you like.

2 Choose two characters from the film and act out a scene with these characters in it.

3 Present it to another pair.

4 The others will ask questions to find out who you are.
Example:
Are you young or old? – Yes, I am./No, I'm not.
Have you got dark hair? – Yes, I have./No, I haven't.

5 Tune in Discussion

1 Who are the people in the photographs?

2 📟 **Listen. Which of the people are the teenagers talking about?**

3 Match the positive and negative sentences.

1 She's very pretty.
2 She's got a great voice.
3 She's a great actress.

a She's got a terrible voice.
b She's ugly.
c She can't act.

⟫⟫ 12 p121

6 Language study

Agreeing and disagreeing

	Kim Basinger	Tom Cruise	Sylvester Stallone
Susan	✔	✔	✗
Tony	✔	✗	✗

1 Use the information in the table to find what Susan says to Tony. Match the statements and replies.

Example: 1 - *b*

Susan
1 I really like Tom Cruise.
2 I think Kim Basinger is great.
3 Tom Cruise is very talented.
4 Kim Basinger is beautiful.
5 I don't like Sylvester Stallone.

Tony
a I agree.
b I don't agree.
c So do I.
d I don't think so.
e Neither do I.

2 Write your own sentences about these people and read them to your partner. Does your partner agree?

7 A survey Favourites

1 Look at the results of a class survey. Who is your favourite actor/actress?

	boys	girls
Tom Cruise	1	52
Kim Basinger	18	2
Sylvester Stallone	12	1
Eddie Murphy	8	3
Julia Roberts	5	2

2 In turns, tell the others who your favourite actor/actress is and give two reasons why he/she is your favourite. Each person in the group says whether they agree with your choice and your reasons.
Example:
I think Eddie Murphy is a good actor.
– So do I./I don't think so.
He is very funny. – I agree./I don't agree.

3 Think about your favourite film character. Talk about him/her.

8 Words...words...words

1 Find the opposites of these words.
Example: *kind - unkind*

kind friendly intelligent interesting generous hard-working helpful	unfriendly boring unkind mean unhelpful lazy stupid

2 Describe two members of your family with these words.
Example:
My brother is intelligent and helpful.

9 Dictation

A Turn to PAIRWORK A8 p103
B Turn to PAIRWORK B7 p110

10 Spot check

Write an appropriate question or statement for each of these replies.
Example:
No, I don't. *Do you play tennis during the week?*

1 I agree.
2 Yes, I did.
3 So do I.
4 No, I haven't.
5 Neither do I.
6 Yes, I do.

WRITING *Film reviews*

1 What types of film are reviewed?

science fiction   western
detective   comedy
adventure   horror   romance

2 Match the comments to the correct review.

1 It's a funny film, but it also has a lot of action for all of you muscle fans!
2 It's an exciting movie, full of action and atmosphere.

3 Can you find an example of these tenses in each review?

1 present simple
2 present continuous
3 simple past

4 Find words in the reviews which mean the same as:

1 group
2 fight
3 destroy
4 finds out

5 Write a review of a film you like and include a picture or a photograph. Present your review like this:

Film:
Best actor:
Star rating:
The story:

Comment:

FILM   Robin Hood: Prince of Thieves

Best actor: Kevin Costner and Christian Slater

Star rating: ★★★★

The story: The story takes place in England hundreds of years ago. The Sheriff of Nottingham takes Robin Hood's land. Robin lives in the forest and steals from the rich to give to the poor. He has a band of people who help him in his battle against the evil Sheriff. He also falls in love with Maid Marion. At the end of the film Robin recovers his land and marries Maid Marion.

Comment:........................

FILM   Kindergarten Cop

Best actor: Arnold Schwarzenegger

Star rating: ★★★

The story: A tough American policeman goes undercover as a kindergarten teacher. He is trying to break a criminal gang. At first, he finds that life in the classroom is more difficult than life on the dangerous city streets. At the end of the film he arrests the criminals and discovers that he enjoys working with children.

Comment:...

UNIT 7 — A helping hand

1 WESTGATE KIDS
EPISODE 3

1 🔲 Listen. Who is not going on the school trip?

1 Hi, Mike.
Hi, Dave.

2 Are you going on the school trip next week?
No, I'm playing with my band on Friday.

3 Great! So why the long face?
I've got problems at home.

4 Dave, over here!
Look, there's Susan.

5 Call me tonight.
He's really depressed.

6 He never smiles or says hello.
Let's forget it! What about the school trip?
I'm not going. Matt's taking me to the cinema.

7 Not Matt Wilkins who left last year!
Yeah, that's right.

8 You're joking! He's a real trouble-maker.
I don't care and anyway you don't know him.

9 I know he's been in trouble with the police!
He's jealous!

2 Are these statements true or false?
1 Mike is playing with his band on Saturday.
2 Mike is very friendly to Susan.
3 Susan is going to the cinema with Dave.

3 Listen and then act out the scenes.

>>> 13 p121

2 Language study
Talking about future arrangements

1 **Which tense is used in each of these sentences?**

1 Dave is going on the school trip next week.
2 Dave is talking to Susan at the moment.

2 **What time do each of the sentences refer to: present or future?**

3 **Complete these sentences with the correct form of the verbs in brackets.**

1 Mike (meet) Dave tonight.
2 Mike (play) with his band on Friday.
3 Mike and Susan (not go) on the school trip next week.
4 Matt (take) Susan to the cinema next week.

4 **Use these expressions to ask about your partner's plans.**

tonight   next week   on Friday
Example:
tonight *What are you doing tonight?*
– I'm playing tennis with Peter.

3 Game Arrangements

1 Copy the table.

	John	Mary	David	Helen	Paul
Monday					
Tuesday					
Wednesday					
Thursday					
Friday					

2 Write these arrangements in different squares for each of the people.

go to a disco
visit grandparents
go to the country
play basketball
meet friends

3 Work in groups. In turns, find out what other students have arranged for the people in the table.
Example:
What is Mary doing on Thursday?
– She's visiting her grandparents.

4 You win ten points for every arrangement which is the same as yours.

4 Mike's busy week

1 🔲 **Listen. Does Mike remember the appointments in his diary correctly?**

1 Monday
St. David's Day
Meet Paula at The Snack Shop – 7 p.m.

2 Tuesday
DENTIST – 11 a.m.

3 Wednesday
Ember Day
Terry's house in evening

4 Thursday
Help mum with shopping (after school)

5 Friday
Ember Day
playing with the band

6 Saturday
Ember Day
football at 10 a.m.
Meet Brenda at Tiffany's – 8 p.m.

7 Sunday
Lent 2
Purim
visit grandparents

2 Write sentences about Mike's week with the correct information.
Example:
He is not meeting Paula at the cinema at 8 p.m. He is meeting her at The Snack Shop at 7 p.m.

3 Find out what your partner is doing next week. Write his/her diary.
Example:
What are you doing on Monday?
– I'm going to the cinema.

4 Who has the most interesting week?

5 Pairwork Puzzle it out

Ａ Turn to PAIRWORK A9 p104
Ｂ Turn to PAIRWORK B8 p111

6 Tune in Sorry!

PARTY!
Bring a friend
Saturday 4pm till late!

1 🔊 **Listen. How does Joan feel at the end of the calls: happy, angry or sad?**

2 What excuses do people make?

1 Jenny	visiting grandparents
2 Fred	playing football
3 Harry	going out for a meal
4 Pat	going shopping

14 p121

7 Language study Excuses

1 Study this:

A: Can you come round to my house tomorrow evening?
B: No, I can't tomorrow, but I can come on Wednesday.
C: I'm sorry, I can't. I'm going to the cinema.

2 Complete the dialogue with the correct form of can.

A: Do you want to go to a disco with me on Friday?
B: I'm sorry, I ____. I'm visiting my grandparents.
A: Well, ____ you go on Saturday at eight?
B: No, I ____ go at eight. ____ we go later?
A: OK. That's fine!

3 Practise the dialogue in pairs.

8 Sounds right

1 🔊 **Listen to these sounds.**
1 /ɑː/   2 /æ/   3 /ə/

2 Which sound do you hear in the underlined words.
1 Can you go out tonight? No, I can't.
2 I can't go out tonight. I'm busy.
3 I can go out tomorrow.

3 Listen and repeat.

9 Role play On the phone

1 Unjumble the speech bubbles to find the dialogue.

Do you want to go to the cinema on Friday?
Hello, 344 7898.
Hi Mary, this is Paul.
Fine. See you then.
What about Saturday?
I'm sorry but I can't. My gran's visiting us.
Yes, OK. What time?
At six at your house.
Hi, Paul.

2 Write a telephone conversation for this situation. Act it out.

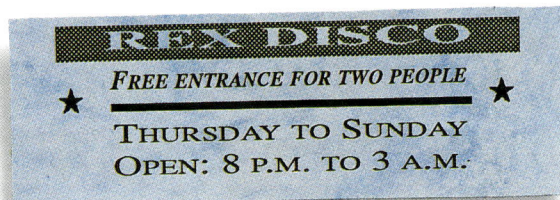

REX DISCO
FREE ENTRANCE FOR TWO PEOPLE
★ THURSDAY TO SUNDAY
OPEN: 8 P.M. TO 3 A.M.

10 Spot check

1 Work in pairs. Find examples of the present continuous in the dialogue.

J: Hi, Mary. What are you doing?
M: I'm working.
J: With your bicycle?
M: Yes, I'm a paper girl.
J: What are you doing tonight?
M: I'm going to the cinema with Tim. What about you?
J: I'm not doing anything.
M: Do you want to come?
J: Yeah!

2 Which examples refer to the present and which to the future?

ASSIGNMENT 4

What's on?

1 READING

How many differences are there between the advertisement and the article about the tour?

2 LISTENING *Dates*

🔊 Listen. Copy and complete the table with the dates.

	dates
Dire Straits Concert	
Charity Concert	
FA Cup Final	
European Athletics Final	
Hard Rock Premiere	

3 VOCABULARY *Brainstorming*

1 Which of the words do you associate with a disco?
sleep hot cold quiet noise friends
music Friday night

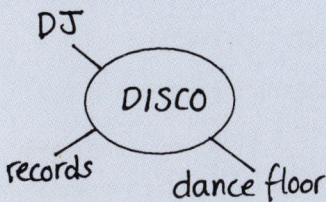

DJ
DISCO
records   dance floor

2 Brainstorm three more words you associate with a disco.

3 In pairs, brainstorm words for the following:
1 Saturday night
2 School

BANDSTAND and ANDREW MILLER proudly present

STING

NOVEMBER

● **Friday 22nd**
ABERDEEN EXHIBITION AND
CONFERENCE CENTRE
Tickets £15.50.
Start 7.30 p.m. Credit
card hotline: 031 557 696.
Tickets available from
Aberdeen Box Office, Union
Street (0224 6412) and all
usual agents.

● **Saturday 23rd**
SCOTTISH EXHIBITION AND
CONFERENCE CENTRE
Tickets £15.50/£12.50.
Start 8 p.m. Credit card
hotline: 031 556 454.
Tickets available from all
TOCTA agents.

● **Monday 25th**
WHITLEY BAY ICE RINK
Tickets £13.00.
Start 7.45 p.m. Tickets
available from Whitley Bay
Box Office and usual agents.

● **Friday
29th/Saturday 30th**
WEMBLEY ARENA
Tickets £17.50/£15.50.
Start 7 p.m. Tickets
available from: Wembley
Arena Box Office, Virgin
Megastore, Oxford Street
Albarmare, Premier,
Stargreen, Ticketmaster.

ALL TICKETS SUBJECT
TO BOOKING FEE

Sting is doing an impressive tour of Great Britain. He is giving five major concerts in November. The first is in Aberdeen on Thursday 22nd. Tickets for the concerts are selling for less than £14, so we are expecting fans from all over the country to come. After Aberdeen, he is playing in Whitley on Friday 23rd and then on Monday 26th at the Scottish Exhibition and Conference Centre. He is giving his final concert of the month at Wembley Arena. You can buy your tickets for £15 from all TOCTA agents or call 071 901 123 to buy your ticket by credit card.

4 FOLLOW UP *A poster*

1 Design a poster for one of these events.
1 a rock concert tour (starting next week)
2 a new cinema (opening next month)
3 a new disco (opening tomorrow)

2 Write a note to a friend inviting him/her to come.

Review and Extension 2

1 Grammar

■ Comparison

1 Which school subjects do you like? Copy the table and mark each subject from 1 to 5 (1 = maximum, 5 = minimum).

	useful	easy	boring	fun
1 English				
2 mathematics				
3 history				
4 art				
5 science				

2 Compare your table with your partner's.
Example:
I think mathematics is more useful than art. Science is the most useful.

3 Choose a topic to make a table.
1 Entertainment - television, books, plays, films, radio
2 Sport - tennis, swimming, basketball, athletics

4 Ask your partner to complete the table.

5 In pairs, discuss your answers.

■ Short answers

Work in pairs. What questions can you ask your partner to receive these answers?
1 Yes, I am.
2 No, I'm not.
3 Yes, I do.
4 No, I don't.
5 Yes, I did.
6 No, I didn't.

■ Future arrangements

1 Write down three plans you have made for different days next week.
Example:
next Tuesday - go swimming

2 Find two people in the class to do these things with you.
Example:
A: *What are you doing on Tuesday?*
 B: *Nothing.*
A: *Do you want to go swimming with me?*

2 Vocabulary

Copy and complete the table with these words.
fan   on Saturday   tomorrow   evening   cinema   star   morning   next week   actor

time	films

3 In conversation

1 Work in pairs. Say these expressions in your language.

1. John's having a birthday party next Saturday.
2. Are you going?
3. I can't. I'm going to the cinema.
4. Can I help you?
5. What about a pair of trainers?
6. Have you got anything cheaper?
7. I don't like this pair.
8. Neither do I.
9. I think he'll like these.
10. Why don't we try a different shop?

2 You are out shopping for your best friend's birthday present. Use five of these expressions in a dialogue.

3 Act out your dialogue for another pair.

4 Study skills Assessing progress

1 Copy the table and mark each item from 1 to 5 (1 = maximum, 5 = minimum).

	how I feel about ...	priorities for next term ...
vocabulary		
grammar		
speaking		
listening		
reading		
writing		

2 Compare your table with your partner's.

1 The adventure diary

Work in your adventure teams. Complete the diary with *is* or *are*.

Day 1
The storm [1] _____ getting worse and worse. It [2] _____ dark and we [3] _____ both tired.

Day 2
The weather [4] _____ changing. There [5] _____ no wind and we [6] _____ drifting helplessly. We do not have any water. The sun [7] _____ hot and we [8] _____ both thirsty.

Day 3
The next thing we remember [9] _____ waking up on a beach. The boat [10] _____ missing. We [11] _____ alone on a desert island – or at least we think we [12] _____ alone!

2 Voices

Listen. What do the teenagers decide to do?
1 wait on the beach
2 go towards the centre of the island
3 make a raft to escape

3 Investigate *Life in the sea*

Turn to Investigation file 2 p116

37

Animal magic!

1 Dr Rufus' laboratory

1 Read the story. What happens to the children?

Dr Rufus is a scientist. He is working on a new potion that will change people into animals.

Dad has left us a note.

Wally and Shirlie, Please be good. And remember, don't go into the laboratory! Love, Dad

Wow, look at all these buttons!

What'll happen if I press this red one?

You shouldn't ...

Oh no, a black cat! That's unlucky.

Don't be silly! Come on.

Wally, what are you doing?

I'm looking for a drink. I'm thirsty.

If I mix these ... mmm, it's delicious ...

Give me some!

Oh dear Wally, you don't look well.

What's happening?

I feel sick and ... aaagh ...

Oh no, my beautiful laboratory - destroyed!

Later that evening ...

And the children! Where are the children?

Woof, woof. Hi, dad! Woof ...

2 🎦 **Listen to complete the sentences.**
1 If you drink the antidote quickly, ...
2 If you look at the full moon, ...
3 If you turn into dogs again, ...
4 If you don't carry garlic, ...
5 If you go out alone at night, ...

⟫⟫ 15 p121

2 Language study
First conditional

1 Match the two parts of the sentences to find some British superstitions.
1 If a spider walks across your hand,...
2 If you walk under a ladder,...
3 If you touch a black cat,...
4 If you break a mirror,...
... you'll have seven years' bad luck.
... you'll have good luck.
... you'll have an unlucky day.
... you'll make a lot of money.

2 Complete the boxes.

possible condition		possible result
If + _____ ,	+	_____ + infinitive without *to*

3 Write three of your country's superstitions.

4 Study this:
What'll happen if I press this red one?

Write questions for each of the superstitions in Part 1.

3 What about you?

1 Write answers for these questions.
What will happen if ...
1 you do not do your homework for tomorrow?
2 you arrive home late without a reason?
3 you do not eat your dinner tonight?
4 you kiss your best friend's boy/girlfriend?
5 a dog bites you?
6 it rains on the way home?

2 Ask your partner the questions. What is the worst thing that will happen?

4 Role play Dialogues

1 Jenny is going on a safari next week and her friend is asking her some questions about it. Complete the friend's questions and then write Jenny's answers using the pictures and the prompts.

Example:
a lion attacks you
What'll you do if a lion attacks you?
climb a tree *I'll climb a tree.*

1 see an elephant
take a photo

2 a rhinoceros chases you
hide behind a rock

3 get lost
shout for help

4 a snake bites you
go to the doctor

5 do not like the food
take sandwiches

2 Practise the dialogues in pairs.

5 Tune in The pet vet

1 📷 **Write the names of four pets you know.**

2 Listen. Which pet is mentioned?

3 Listen again. Are the statements true or false?

- You should not keep a python if you have other pets.
- Pythons sleep a lot.
- You should keep your python in a warm part of the house.
- You should feed your python a live mouse once a week.
- You should never wash your hands before you touch your python.
- Pythons do not need much exercise.

▶▶▶ **16** p121

6 Language study

Giving advice

1 Complete the text with *should* and *should not*.

> What 1_____ you do if you want to buy a goldfish? First of all, you 2_____ buy a bowl big enough for it. You 3_____ also change the water every two weeks. And remember do not feed it too much! You 4_____ feed it more than twice a day, and then only a little at a time.

2 Your friend wants to buy a cat. What advice can you give him/her?

3 How are statements, questions and negatives formed with *should*?

7 Dictation Puzzle

Work in pairs to find the secret code.

🗣 **A** Turn to PAIRWORK A10 p104
👥 **B** Turn to PAIRWORK B9 p111

8 A day at the zoo

1 Work in pairs. What advice would you give to the people in the picture?

- touch the snakes
- put your fingers into the monkeys' cage
- feed the lions
- leave your baby alone
- climb trees
- take your dog's lead off

2 What advice would you give to people who live in a city?

9 Sounds right

1 📷 **Listen to these sounds.**

/ʃ/	/tʃ/

2 Put the words into the appropriate column.
shark cheetah children should machine musician delicious future picture shop wash match

3 Work in pairs to play Sharks and Cheetahs.

4 Read these sentences quickly to your partner. Do not read the words containing the sounds /ʃ/ or /tʃ/. For a word containing /ʃ/ read *sharks* and a word containing /tʃ/ read *cheetahs*.

> In future the children should wash after going to the match. We have a delicious lunch prepared for them and afterwards they can listen to the musicians or go to the shops to buy some pictures.

10 Spot check

Find examples of the first conditional (statements, questions and negatives) from this unit.

ASSIGNMENT 5
Animal care

1 READING *A day in the park*

1 Do you have any pets?

2 In your opinion, what type of pet is the most difficult to look after?

3 Read the story. What does Tommy do wrong?

Here you are, Tommy. And remember, you shouldn't take his lead off.

Don't worry Gran, I won't.

Mmm, it's empty. If I take his lead off for a moment, nothing will happen.

PARK KEEP DOGS ON LEAD

Oh, no! Blackie, Blackie! Here!

Woof, woof.

Good dog. Aaagh!

Woof, grr ...

ten minutes later

I'm really sorry. He's a good dog but ...

2 LISTENING *Quantities*

1 🔊 Listen. Which quantities do you hear?

half a kilo 3 kilos 100 grams 2 kilos 5 litres
15 grams 500 grams 4 litres 150 grams

2 Match the abbreviations to the words.

kg	pound
lb	gram
oz	kilo
g	ounce

3 Write these quantities in words.

Example:
3½ kg = *three and a half kilos*
500 g = ____ ____ grams
2 ½ lb= ____ ____ ____ ____ pounds
8 ¼ lb = ____ ____ ____ ____ pounds
7 oz = ____ ____
6 ¾ lb = ____ ____ ____ ____ ____

3 VOCABULARY
Index cards

1 Complete the index card with these expressions.

leave it alone in the car
brush it regularly
let it bark at people

2 Make an index card with the heading *English*. Say what you should and should not do to learn English.

4 FOLLOW UP *Investigate*

1 Choose a pet. Write sentences about what you should and should not do to look after it properly.

2 Compare what you wrote with another student.

Problem page

1 Dear Ruby

1 Read the letters to Ruby's problem page. Match the titles to the letters.

1 *I'm bored.*

2 *I'm worried.*

3 *I'm fed up.*

4 *I'm not stupid!*

A Dear Ruby,
I've got problems at school. I've failed my exams twice. My father has decided to help me by asking me questions every night. He even asks me questions during dinner! I know he's trying to help, but I hate it!
Yours,
Unhappy

B Dear Ruby,
I've never had a real girlfriend. I'm sixteen. I'm tall and my friends think I'm good-looking. I have a lot of friends - some of them girls, but there is no-one special! Is there something wrong with me?
Yours,
Puzzled

C Dear Ruby,
Have you ever eaten cold spaghetti? I have - it's horrible! In fact I eat it at school every Thursday. Last week I was nearly sick. I've told my dad but he thinks I'm being fussy. I don't know what to do!
Yours,
Sickly

D Dear Ruby,
My mum's just got a new job and we've moved town. It's terrible. I haven't got any friends and the town is boring. What happens here? Let me tell you - nothing! I'm going mad. What should I do?
Yours,
Desperate

2 Match these extracts from Ruby's replies to three of the letters above.

1 ■ No, I haven't! Have you talked to your teachers? If you explain the problem, they'll probably make sure your food is 'good and hot' next week!

2 ■ Have you tried visiting the local youth club? I'm sure when you meet some local teenagers they'll show you how to have a good time there.

3 ■ Have you asked anyone to go out with you? You probably haven't met the girl of your dreams. I really don't understand the problem! Tall, handsome and sixteen you sound wonderful! Be patient and I'm sure you'll find a special friend.

3 📼 Look at the letters again. Listen to find who is speaking.

4 Listen again. Copy and complete the table.

	yes	no	when
started school			
joined the youth club			
joined a sports club			

>>> 17 p121

42

2 Language study
Present perfect simple

1 Study this:

indefinite past time	definite past time
I have eaten cold spaghetti.	I ate cold spaghetti last week.

2 Match each example to a column.
1 I've never been to France.
2 I went to Paris last year.
3 When did you go to Milan?
4 I've visited England twice.
5 I went to England in 1990.
6 I haven't heard the new Prince CD.
7 I heard Prince's new CD ten days ago.
8 Have you ever been to Italy?

3 Look at the letters to Ruby. Find more examples of sentences in the past.

4 Write a list of four interesting experiences you have had in your life.
Example:
climbed a mountain/ flown in a plane/ eaten a curry/ been abroad

5 Has your partner had the same experiences? If the answer is *Yes*, ask when.
Example:
A: *Have you ever climbed a mountain?*
B: *Yes, I have.*
A: *When did you climb it?*
B: *Last summer.*

3 Role play   Experience wanted

A Turn to PAIRWORK A11 p104
B Turn to PAIRWORK B10 p111

4 Game Round in circles

1 Work in groups. Copy the circles.

FOOD

MUSIC

PLACES

FILMS

BOOKS

SPORT

PETS

2 Throw a coin to move (*heads* two circles; *tails* one circle).

3 Ask someone a question about the circle you land on.
Example:
Have you ever visited Brussels?

4 If the answer is *Yes* you win five points.

43

5 Tune in Helpline

1 🔊 **How would you describe each of the callers?**

angry   sad   happy   puzzled

2 What did each caller phone about?

First caller: a) has just lost her little dog
b) has just won a lot of money
Second caller: a) has just failed his exams
b) has just lost his job
Third caller: a) has just failed her exams
b) has just lost her little dog
Fourth caller: a) has just lost his job
b) has just won a lot of money

▶▶ 18 p121

6 Language study

Talking about present results

1 Match past actions to present results.

past action	present result
1 She did the football pools.	a He has broken his leg.
2 He fell over.	b He has broken the window.
3 He kicked the ball hard.	c She has won the football pools.

2 Look at the pictures showing present result. Think of what each person is saying and write a sentence for each picture.
Example:
a win the pools
I've won the pools.
b break a leg
c break a window

7 Pairwork Identical twins

👥 A Turn to PAIRWORK A12 p104
B Turn to PAIRWORK B11 p111

8 Game Something to smile about

Work in groups.

 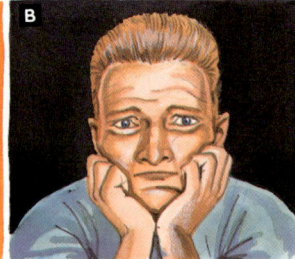

1 Write three sentences about what has just happened to these people to make them smile or frown.
Example:
a) *She has just won the football pools.*

2 Read one of your sentences to the group.

3 In turns, you should smile or frown when you hear a sentence. You should smile if the sentence is positive and frown if the sentence is negative.

4 If you smile or frown when you should not, you are out of the game.

9 Dictation

👥 A Turn to PAIRWORK A13 p105
B Turn to PAIRWORK B12 p111

10 Spot check

1 Copy and complete the table.

infinitive	simple past	past participle
be	was/were	been
eat		eaten
win	won	
break		

2 Add four more verbs to the table.

3 Write sentences about yourself with two of the verbs.
Example:
I have been to London. I was there last year.

WRITING *A letter to a friend*

1 Answer these questions.
1 Where do you put your address and the date in an informal letter?
2 Should you write your name at the top?
3 How should you begin and end the letter?

2 Read the letter to check.

3 Answer these questions.
1 Where is Pedro?
2 What has he done in London?
3 What is the problem?

4 Which piece of advice is the best for him?
1 Have you tried talking to the hotel manager?
2 You should try eating in different restaurants.
3 You should not complain about the food.

5 Use these prompts to write another letter.

Palace Hotel
23 Stanley Place
London

7th August 1993

Dear Juan,

London is wonderful! We've already seen hundreds of interesting places and we've been very busy.

Last Tuesday we spent the day at the Tower of London. It was great – we saw all the Queen's jewels. It's definitely my favourite place. Yesterday we visited Buckingham Palace and Westminster Abbey and we had a picnic in Hyde Park. I've taken lots of photos to show you when we get back.

The only problem is the food in the hotel – it's terrible! We're always hungry and eat lots of snacks.

Anyway, see you soon.

Love,
Pedro

Eiffel
12 River Bank
Paris

17th August 1993

Dear David,

Paris /be/ wonderful! We /already/see/ hundreds of interesting places and so far we/eat/ a lot.

Last Wednesday /we/spend/ the day at Versailles. It/be/great. We/visit/ the palace and the beautiful gardens as well. It/be/definitely my favourite place. Yesterday /we/go/ to the Champs-Elysées and the Eiffel Tower. I/take/lots of photos to show you when/ we/get back.

The only problem /be/ our hotel. The people in the next room /watch/ television till 2 a.m. and /it/be/ impossible to sleep!

Anyway, see you soon.

Love,

Paula

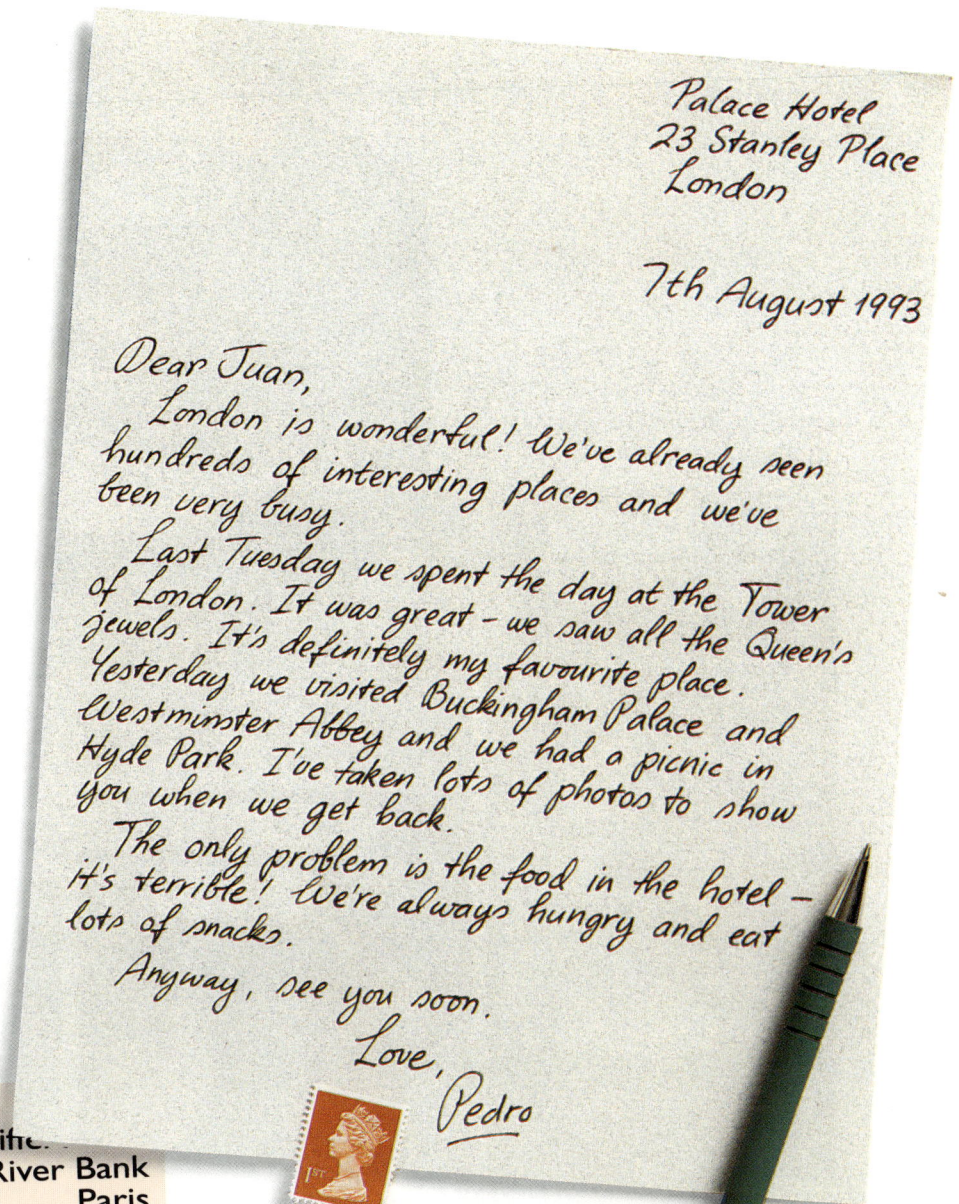

6 Write your own letter from a different place. Include a problem. Give it to another student to read. Has he/she got any interesting advice for you?

45

In trouble

It's ten past eight and Mike's not here yet.

2 *I'm leaving, he's an hour late.*

1 WESTGATE KIDS
EPISODE 4

1 Look at the first two pictures. Why do you think Mike is late? Listen to check.

3 *Where have you been? I have to be home by ten!*

4 *What have you got your bag for?*

5 *What was the argument about?*

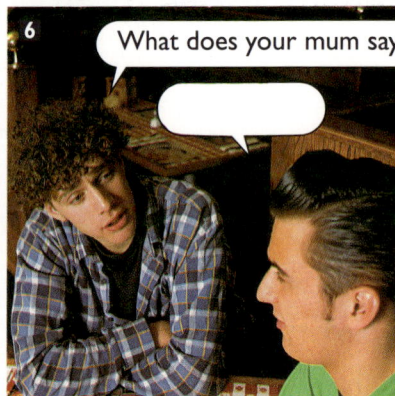

6 *What does your mum say?*

Have you tried talking to them?

7

8 *Be honest!*

9 *OK, but only tonight. And tell them where you are.*

2 Match what Mike says to the correct scenes in the story.

- Well, I need time to think. Can I stay at your place tonight? I'm not going to go back home tonight.
- She's worried. They both work and I have to look after my younger brothers, but I want to live my own life.
- Look, I'm really sorry.
- I had an argument with my dad.
- It's not that easy. What do I say?
- Yeah, OK. I'll phone later.
- Everything - school, home, my band - I can't do my own thing.

3 Practise the dialogue in pairs.

>>> 19 p121

2 Language study Intentions

1 When does Mike decide to leave home? Before he meets Dave or while he is speaking?

2 When does Mike decide to phone home? Before he meets Dave or while he is speaking?

3 What is the difference between *going to* and *will* to express future intention?

4 Match the sentences to *a* or *b*.
a spontaneous decision
b planned action

1 I'm not going to lend it to you any more.
2 I'll meet you at eight.
3 I'm going to study harder.
4 I'll never do that again!

5 Think of a humorous situation for each sentence. Use these ideas to help you.
a Who is the speaker?
b Who is he/she speaking to?
c What is the situation?
Example:

1 I'm not going to lend it to you any more.
a *Michael Jackson.*
b *His pet monkey, Bubbles.*
c *Bubbles has broken his personal stereo twice this week.*

3 Game Intentions circle

| You have the day off school tomorrow. | You win £1,000.. | You get a free ticket to London. |

1 Work in groups. Student A reads a card.
Example:
You win £1,000.

2 Student B decides what he/she will do.
Example:
I'll buy a motorbike.

3 Student C decides what he/she will do and reports Student B's decision as well.
Example:
I'll visit Paris. Peter's going to buy a motorbike.

4 The game continues round the group until everyone has made and reported a decision.

4 Role play Dialogues

1 🔲 Copy the table and listen to complete it.

	Tom	Mary	Sally
make the sandwiches			
buy the drinks			
phone friends			
bring the music			
make the invitations			

2 Work in groups. Organise a class party.
Example:
A: *I'll make the invitations.*
B: *OK, and I'll decorate the room.*

3 Report what you are going to do to another group.
Example:
John is going to bring the records. Mary and Dan are going to make a cake.

4 Who is going to organise the best party?

5 Tune in Jobs at home

1 📷 **Listen to Bill and Richard. Copy and complete the table showing what they have to (✔) and don't have to (✗) do.**

	Bill	Richard
make bed		
tidy room		
put clothes away		
cook		
lay table		
put rubbish out		
wash dishes		
sweep floor		
go shopping		

2 Copy these sentences. Listen again to complete them.
1 What do you ____ ____ do?
2 I ____ ____ make my ____ and ____ my room.
3 I don't ____ ____ ____ anything in the kitchen.
4 I often ____ ____ ____ shopping.

>> 20 p121

6 Language study Obligation

1 What is the difference between *have* and *have to* in these sentences?

1 I have a bicycle.
2 I have to go to bed early.

2 What is the difference between these sentences?
1 I have to go to school on Saturday.
2 I don't have to go school on Saturday.

3 Work in groups. Write a list of things you have to and don't have to do at school.

have to	don't have to
go to class on time	wear a uniform

4 In your groups, ask your teacher about your notes to check.
Example:
Do we have to go to class on time? – Yes, you do.
Do we have to wear a uniform? – No, you don't.

7 Survey Life at home

1 Make a table like the one in Activity 5.

2 Interview three students in your class.
Example:
Do you have to make your bed?
– Yes, I do. / No, I don't.

3 Write sentences about one of the people you interviewed.
Example:
George has to make his bed, but he does not have to put the rubbish out.

8 Game People and jobs

1 Work in groups.

2 Turn to PAIRWORK A14 p105

9 Sounds right

1 📷 **Listen to these sounds.**
1 /v/   2 /f/

2 Listen to find the sounds in the text.

I live with my family in a lovely house and I have a room of my own. I have to tidy it every day. I have a lot of different things in my room. I have a bed, a wardrobe, a table and a very small television. I don't have to go to bed early, but sometimes I watch television in bed.

3 Read the text to your partner.

10 Spot check

Find two examples in the unit for each of the following:
1 spontaneous decision
2 planned action
3 obligation
4 no obligation

Arguments

1 READING *Reports*

I Read these headings.
Us v. them
A parent looks back
An unhappy child

2 Read the text quickly and choose the best heading for it.

3 Answer the questions.
I What things do parents and children argue about?
2 What did the writer argue about?
3 Did the writer do what her mother asked?
4 What do her children have to do?
5 What does she smile about?

Teenagers argue with their parents for lots of different reasons. Some argue about clothes, others about jobs in the house, and others about their friends. I remember when I was young. I argued about everything. When my mum asked, 'Have you tidied your room?' I always replied, 'I'm going to tidy it tomorrow!' Of course, tomorrow never came and we had the inevitable argument. Now I have children and they have to do things around the house - usually tomorrow! Sometimes we argue and then I remember the arguments I had with my mother and smile about how little things have changed.

2 LISTENING *Frequency*

I 🔊 Copy the table. Listen to complete it.

2 Write three sentences to say how often you argue with your parents/friends/best friend.

	older brother	little sister	mum	dad	friends	best friend
every day						
quite a lot						
once a week						
now and again						
hardly ever						

3 VOCABULARY *Scales*

I Look at the vocabulary scale.

Arguments at home

always	TV
very often	clothes
often	homework
usually	bedtime
sometimes	music
hardly ever	friends
never	food

2 Make your own argument scale for:
I at home
2 with friends

4 FOLLOW UP *Finding out*

I Choose one of the argument scales and interview three other students in your class.
Example:
What do you argue about at home? – Clothes.
How often do you argue about them? – Well, sometimes.
What else do you argue about?

2 Present your information like this:

```
Name: _____   Date: _____
Names of people interviewed:
1 _____
2 _____
3 _____
Argument scales
1
2
3
```

Food and fitness

1 Exhaustion

1 How many things can you name in the picture?

2 What do you think is wrong with the cyclist?

3 Which of these statements give good advice to an exhausted cyclist?
1 Don't put on extra clothes if it's cold.
2 Keep cycling - you'll soon feel better.
3 Stop cycling and rest.
4 Drink a little water.
5 Cycle home quickly.

4 Read the first part of the text to find the answers.

5 Find the names of these foods in the second part of the text.

6 Listen. Which pictures describe the story?

BURN OUT!

Mountain bike riding can be lots of fun, but take our advice - don't be fanatical! There are several important points to remember when you go cycling:
▶ Cycle on routes where there isn't much traffic.
▶ Take a few extra clothes to put on if it's cold and don't stay in the sun if it's hot.
▶ If you feel very tired or confused, stop immediately and have a rest. Drink a little water and relax for about 30 minutes. Then cycle home slowly. You shouldn't try to continue your journey.

▶ You should make sure you drink plenty of water when you go out on your bike. On a hot day your body needs more than a litre of water an hour. If there aren't many places to stop on your route, take lots of bottles of water with you.
▶ Eat a good breakfast before starting. You should try to include brown bread, yoghurt, honey and a lot of fruit. People often ask us, 'How much should we eat when we go cycling?' The answer is, 'A little and often'. You should include these foods in your diet: bananas, nuts, raisins, potatoes, rice and pasta. If you eat these foods you will have lots of energy.

7 Listen again and write two things the cyclist did wrong.

 p121

2 Language study

Countable and uncountable nouns

1 Look at the text *Burn out* again. Copy and complete the table below with the words for food and drink.

countable	uncountable
bananas	pasta

2 Study these sentences and complete the rule.
- How much water should I drink?
- I don't eat much meat. I prefer fish.
- How many extra clothes should I take?
- There aren't many places to stop.

1 We use *much* with:
a uncountable nouns in questions and negatives
b countable nouns in questions and negatives
c uncountable and countable nouns in questions and negatives
2 We use *many* with:
a uncountable nouns in questions and negatives
b countable nouns in questions and negatives
c uncountable and countable nouns in questions and negatives

3 How many correct sentences can you make?

How	much many	bananas? water? rice? potatoes?

You	should not should	eat drink	a lot of a few a little much many	bananas. water. rice. potatoes.

4 Work in pairs.
A Ask B how much you should eat and drink when you go cycling.
B Give A advice on what to eat and drink when he/she goes cycling.
Example:
A: *What should I drink when I go cycling?*
B: *You should drink a lot of water.*
A: *How much water should I drink?*
B: *A litre every hour.*

3 Sumo

1 What do you know about Sumo wrestlers? Write four questions to find out about a Sumo wrestler's life. Start like this:
1 How much ...?
2 How many ...?
3 How often ...?
4 How long ...?

2 Read the text. Does it answer your questions? Complete it with these words.
three   a lot of   half a kilo
a few   plenty of

Only 1____ people in Japan become professional Sumo wrestlers. It is a difficult sport that needs 2____ dedication and training.
   Sumo wrestlers are very large people. They usually eat 3____ big meals a day. They have an enormous breakfast - four or five eggs and 4____ of rice. For lunch and dinner they eat about a kilo of meat and fish, as well as 5____ vegetables and rice. In total, a Sumo wrestler eats three kilos of rice a day and spends eight hours in the gym.

4 Pairwork Training

A PAIRWORK A15 p105
B PAIRWORK B13 p111

5 Tune in School coach

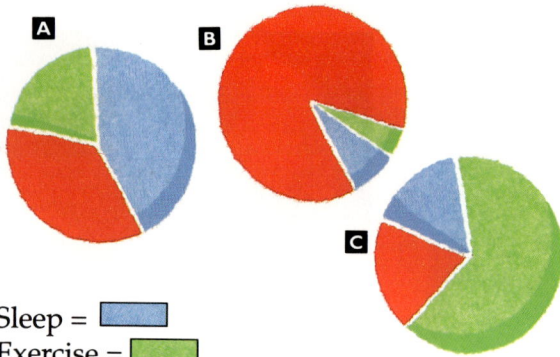

A
B
C

Sleep = ▢
Exercise = ▢
Relaxation/other activity = ▢

🔊 **Listen. Which lifestyle does the coach recommend?**

≫ 22 p121

6 Language study

too much, too many,
too + adjective, not enough

1 🔊 **Listen. Copy and complete the sentences.**
1 This person is having ___ ___ sleep.
2 They are ___ active ___.
3 This person is doing ___ ___ exercise.
4 This person is ___ having ___ sleep.
5 Mentally, they will be ___ ___ to do very much.
6 Now this chart shows a balanced lifestyle: about eight hours sleep a day, not ___ ___ hours exercising.

2 Write sentences for the pictures with *too* and *not enough*.

A
B
C

Example:
a *This person is too fat. He does not do enough exercise.*

7 Find someone who

1 Work in groups. Find someone in your group who ...
... watches too much television.
... eats too much chocolate.
... does not eat enough fruit.
... is usually too busy to do his/her homework.

2 Write about another person in your class.
Example:
David does not watch too much television, but he eats too much chocolate.

8 Role play A visit to the doctor

1 🔊 **Listen. What is the patient's problem?**

1 He has got flu.
2 He has got a stomach-ache.
3 He hasn't got an appetite and sleeps badly.

2 Listen again. Copy the questions and tick (✔) the ones you hear.

What can I do for you?   What's wrong?
Can I help you?   Is that all, doctor?
What do you mean?

3 Work in pairs.

A Turn to PAIRWORK A16 p105
B Turn to PAIRWORK B14 p112

9 Dictation

A Turn to PAIRWORK A17 p105
B Turn to PAIRWORK B15 p112

10 Spot check

1 Are these words used with countable nouns, uncountable nouns or both? Copy the table and tick (✔) the correct boxes.

	countable	uncountable	both
much			
many			
a little			
a few			
a lot of			
plenty of			
not enough			

2 Find an example sentence from the unit for each word and write one example of your own.

WRITING *Guidelines*

1 You are giving advice to someone who wants to keep fit. In pairs, decide what to say about:
1 eating
2 drinking
3 exercise

2 Read the text. Does it give the same advice?

3 You are a doctor. Copy the table and add your advice about keeping fit and healthy.

do	do not
drink lots of water	eat too many snacks

4 Write six sentences as guidelines for your patients.

5 Choose a sport. Write guidelines for someone who wants to start doing it.

GUIDELINES FOR KEEPING FIT

Eating

You should eat a variety of food. You should always have plenty of fish, vegetables and fruit. Eat three meals a day and try not to have too many snacks between meals. Do not eat too much cheese or other dairy products.

Drinking

Drink lots of water and fruit juice. Do not drink too much tea or coffee - it is bad for you! One cup a day is enough.

Exercise

Again, plenty of exercise is healthy, but you also need time to relax and sleep properly. You should do twenty minutes' exercise three times a week - cycling, swimming and jogging are good for you.

Review and Extension 3

1 Grammar

■ First conditional

1 Complete these sentences.
1 If my parents win a lot of money, ...
2 If I pass all my exams, ...
3 If I go to England, ...
4 If it snows all week, ...

2 Complete these sentences.
1 I will cry if you ...
2 I will get angry if you ...
3 I will not be your friend if you ...
4 I will be your friend if you ...

■ Present perfect simple

1 Write questions for these answers.
Example:
Have you ever been abroad?
- Yes, I have. I have been to America.
1 Yes, I have. I have eaten pizza.
2 Yes, I have. I have won two medals.
3 Yes, I have. I have fallen off my bicycle.
4 Yes, I have. I have met Kevin Costner.

2 Write four news items. Think of:
1 the most incredible
2 the funniest
3 the saddest
4 the most probable
Example:
Aliens have just landed in the playground.

Tell two other students. Who has the best news item for each category?

■ *will* and *going to, have to* and *should*

1 Choose a suitable expression to describe each sentence.
no obligation   spontaneous decision   advice
planned action   obligation
1 There is the door bell. I will answer it.
2 I have to study tonight.
3 You should speak more English in class.
4 You do not have to pay to get in.
5 I am going to do more exercise.

2 Write five sentences of your own. Use *will,* *going to, have to* and *should*.

3 Give your sentences to another student. Use one of the expressions from part 1 to describe each sentence.

2 Vocabulary

1 Work in pairs. You have five minutes to add three words to each list.
1 kind   intelligent   3 been   eaten
2 always   often   4 football   tennis

2 Compare your list with that of another pair. Did you write the same words?

3 In conversation

1 Work in pairs. Say these expressions in your language.

1. What should I do?
2. Have you ever been in trouble?
3. What are you going to do tonight?
4. I've lost my exercise book!
5. Do I have to do my homework?
6. I don't have to go home early.
7. I haven't got enough money.
8. Where have you been?
9. You shouldn't do too much exercise.
10. I'll see you tonight.

2 You are having an argument with a friend. Use two or three of these expressions in a dialogue.

3 Act out your dialogue for another pair.

4 Study skills Learning vocabulary

1 Read the questions.
1 How often do you revise new words?
2 How do you revise them?
3 When do you revise them? Where?

2 🔊 **Listen. Which techniques does Rosa use?**
a vocabulary cards
b vocabulary notebook
c word fields
d words with pictures

3 Check your answers in groups.

The Guardians
EPISODE 3

1 The adventure diary

Complete the diary with these words.

did not sleep   are travelling
will find   are going
have decided   do not have enough

Day 4
We ¹ _____ to go towards the centre of the island. If we are lucky we ² _____ people there.

Day 5
We ³ _____ very slowly. The island is a rich tropical forest. Last night we ⁴ _____. The animal noises kept us awake.

Day 6
We ⁵ _____ strength to continue. We ⁶ _____ to make a camp in a clearing and wait for the end!

2 Voices

Listen. Copy the list and number the animals in the order you hear them.

___ elephant   ___ parrot
___ lion   ___ hyena
___ monkey   ___ wolf

3 Investigate *Natural habitat*

Turn to Investigation file 3 p117

55

Suspect

"My life's a real mess!"

1 WESTGATE KIDS
EPISODE 5

1 Read the story. Why do the police want to ask Mike questions?

"Who's that by the school?"

"Why is he going into the school? It's Sunday."

Mike decides to follow

"He's taken the new sports equipment. I'd better call the police!"

"Don't move!"
"But it wasn't me. I ..."

"Come on! Get in the car. We'll talk at the station."
"Oh no! This is all I need!"

2 Listen. Mike is now at the police station. How many questions does the policeman ask?

3 Unjumble the policeman's questions and write Mike's answers.
1 call ? us why you didn't
2 what and you ? did do
3 you him did ? recognise

23 p122

2 Language study Prepositions

1 Match the prepositions to the pictures.
next to   in front of   behind
on   in   into   onto   out of   over   under

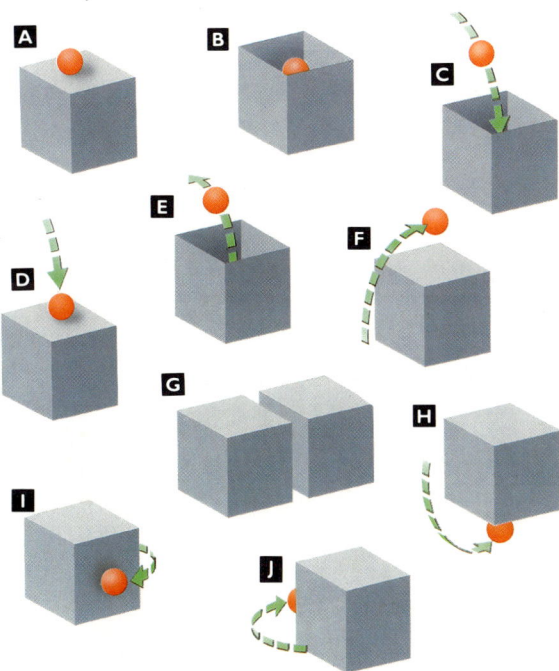

2 Copy and complete the letter with the appropriate prepositions.
on   next to   in   out of   on   under

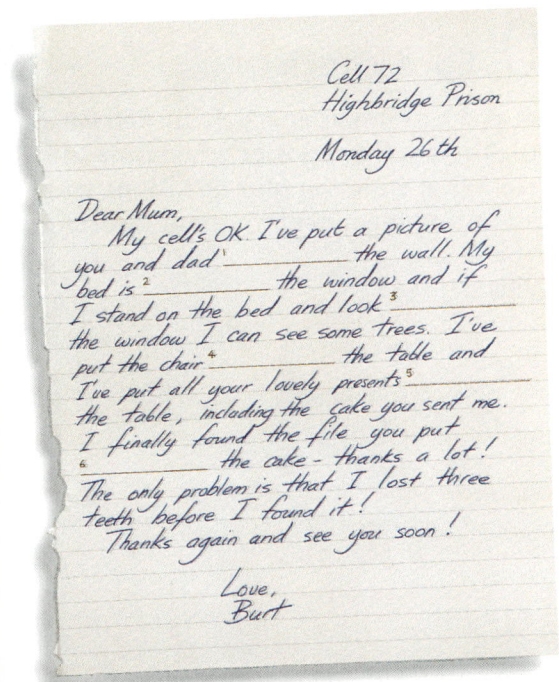

Cell 72
Highbridge Prison

Monday 26th

Dear Mum,
My cell's OK. I've put a picture of
you and dad ¹_____ the wall. My
bed is ²_____ the window and if
I stand on the bed and look ³_____
the window I can see some trees. I've
put the chair ⁴_____ the table and
I've put all your lovely presents ⁵_____
the table, including the cake you sent me.
I finally found the file you put
⁶_____ the cake - thanks a lot!
The only problem is that I lost three
teeth before I found it!
Thanks again and see you soon!

Love,
Burt

3 Draw a diagram of Burt's cell from the description in the letter.

3 A story Escape

You are a policeman. Use the prompts to write your report of the escape. Start like this:
The prisoner was in his cell.

1 climb out of window   2 jump onto roof

3 jump into recreation   4 climb over wall
ground

5 crawl under gate   6 jump into helicopter

4 Pairwork Cat and mouse

A Turn to PAIRWORK A18 p106
B Turn to PAIRWORK B16 p112

5 Tune in The witness

1 📠 **Listen. List the differences between what the speaker says and the newspaper article.**

Yesterday evening two men broke into an off-licence in Leeds. They took more than £2,000, but instead of leaving immediately, they decided to celebrate with a drink. At six o'clock in the morning, the postman noticed a broken window at the back of the shop and called the police. The police arrived and found the two men asleep on the floor with empty bottles of whisky next to them.

2 Match the answers to the question words.

1 two	a What
2 at six o'clock	b How many
3 at the back	c When
4 I'm a postman	d Why
5 because I saw two men asleep	e Where

» 24 p122

6 Language study
Question words

1 Complete these questions with an appropriate verb.
1 _____ you asleep?
2 _____ you got two brothers?
3 _____ you eat meat?

2 Look at your answers. What do you notice about the order of the words? When can we use *do/does/did* to make a question? Write three examples.

3 Complete these questions.
1 Why does your best friend ...?
2 Where were you ...?
3 How much does it ...?
4 What did you ...?
5 When do you ...?

4 Write questions for these answers.
1 £150.
2 At five o'clock.
3 I played football.
4 I'm a student.
5 Last year.
6 On the table.

7 Life in prison

1 Work in groups. You have to spend your life in prison! You can choose the person you share your cell with. Write ten questions to interview people.
Example:
What type of music do you like?

2 Interview the other students in your group and choose the best person.

8 Pairwork Cross examination

A Turn to PAIRWORK A19 p106
B Turn to PAIRWORK B17 p120

9 Sounds right

1 📠 **Listen to the three questions.**
1 What time did you get up yesterday?
2 Who did you see first?
3 Did you eat breakfast?

2 Listen to the next eight questions. Does the voice rise (╱) or fall (╲)?
Example: 1 = ╲

3 Write the questions.

4 In pairs, ask and answer the questions.

10 Spot check

Look at the newspaper article in Activity 5 again. You are the reporter who wrote the article. What were the four questions you asked to find the most important information?
1 What ...?
2 Who ...?
3 Why ...?
4 When ...?

Directions

1 READING
The plan

1 These are the three notes that the police found after a robbery. Study the notes and the map.

2 Copy the map and show the routes the three people took.

3 What do you think happened next? Write an ending for the story.

4 Compare your story with that of another pair. Who wrote the best story?

JOHN
- wait in phone box opposite supermarket
- go along alley behind supermarket
- climb over wall
- break window and go into storeroom
- take money from till near exit
- go to car near exit

SANDRA
- go into supermarket
- collect large amount of shopping
- go to till near entrance
- drop glass bottle at till
- argue with cashier – refuse to pay

DRIVER
- go along Wood Street till you come to the traffic lights
- turn right at the traffic lights
- go straight on, then take the second turning on the left
- the supermarket is on the right
- wait outside

2 LISTENING
Giving directions

1 🔊 Listen. How many times do you hear each of these phrases?

	number of times
1 turn right	
2 turn left	
3 go straight on	
4 opposite	
5 next to	
6 till you get to	

2 Draw a map to show how to get to the disco.

3 VOCABULARY
Prepositions

Work in pairs. How many prepositions can you find in the word square?

```
I N F R O N T O F
N S J M N E S N H
T W B P T X Z J A
O V E R O T G K L
X C H N I T R A T
G S I N M O P T E
V O N T O S L F I
U N D E R G K D A
```

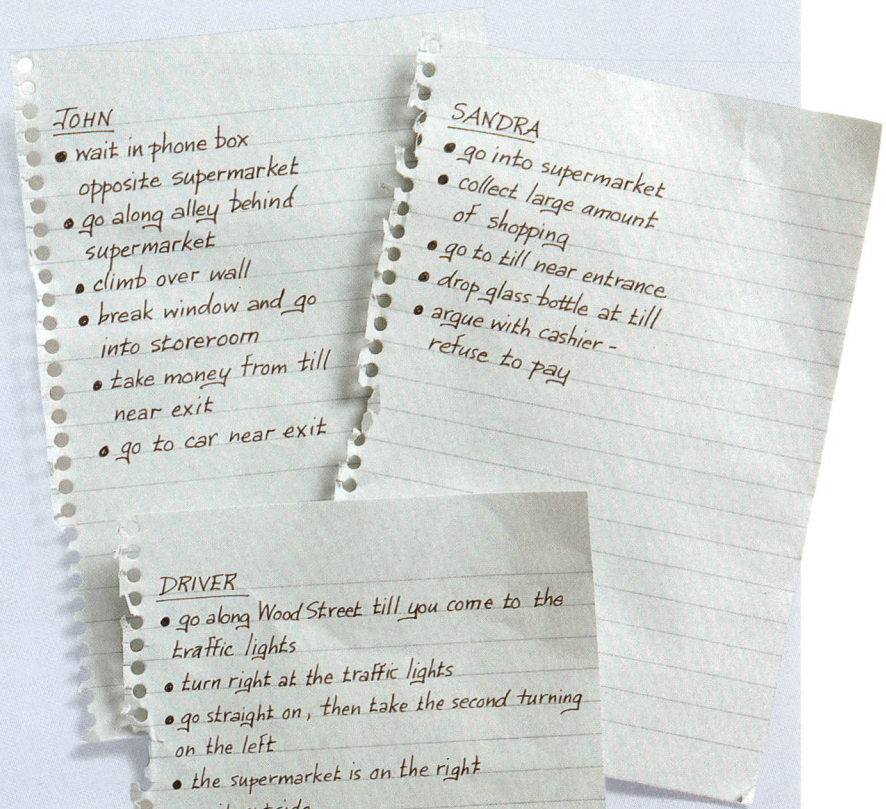

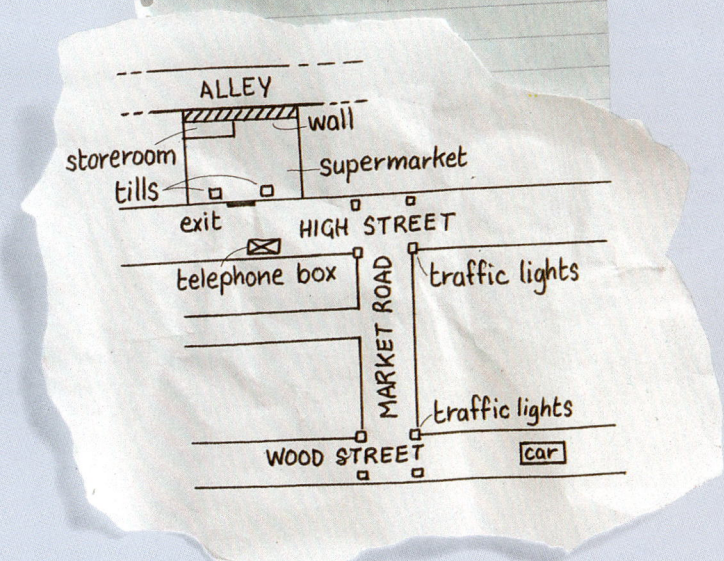

Map labels:
ALLEY
wall
storeroom
supermarket
tills
exit
HIGH STREET
telephone box
MARKET ROAD
traffic lights
traffic lights
WOOD STREET
car

4 FOLLOW UP

1 A friend is staying at your house for the first time. You leave him/her directions explaining how to get from your house to:

a the post office   b a newsagent's   c a bank

2 Draw a map showing the main roads and buildings near your house. Give your directions and the map to another student. Can he/she draw the route on the map?

Fact or fiction

The sun was shining when Carol and Tom arrived at the lake. It was very hot and they both looked at the water which was cool and refreshing.

'Do you want to go for a swim?' asked Tom.

'OK, I'll race you to the island in the middle,' Carol replied.

Tom was the first in the water. He knew that Carol was a better swimmer.

'Wait for me!' Carol shouted.

Carol was swimming towards Tom when suddenly she saw a strange black shape in the water in front of her. It was moving towards Tom, closer and closer.

'Tom!' she screamed.

The black shape was moving quickly. Tom stopped and turned - he was smiling. As he turned to look at Carol, the black shape covered him completely. He disappeared under water. Carol screamed and then there was silence. She was alone.

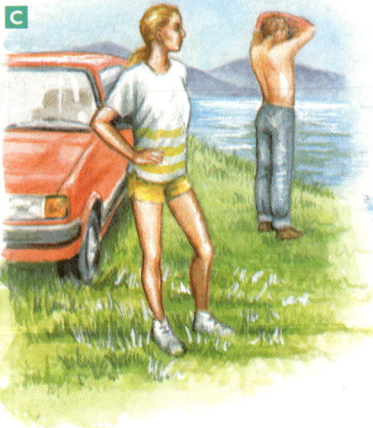

1 Chapter one

1 What type of book do you prefer ?

western   romance   horror
adventure   science fiction

2 What type of book is this passage from?

3 Unjumble the pictures to find the story.

A

B

C

D

E

F

4 Listen. Put these sentences into the correct order.

1 She was crying when she saw a boat.
2 The shape was in the water behind the boat.
3 Carol swam towards the island.
4 The boat was coming towards her.
5 The black shape was waiting in the lake.
6 Carol ran out of the water.

5 Write an ending for the story.

25 p122

2 Language study
Past continuous

1 Name the two tenses in this sentence.
The sun was shining when Carol and Tom arrived at the lake.

2 Which diagram represents the sentence?

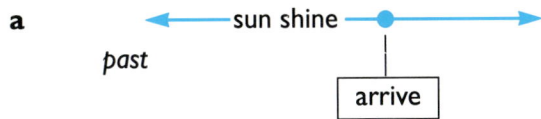

a
sun shine
past
arrive

b
arrive
past
sun shine

3 Use the prompts to write sentences about Sarah's dream.
Example:
Sarah was reading when the phone rang.

a read book/ phone ring
b speak friend/ lights go out

c look for switch/ hear scream
d run away from ghost/wake up

4 Describe Sarah's dream to your partner.

3 Find someone who

Work in groups. Find someone in your group who ...
... was speaking English ten minutes ago.
... was eating breakfast at eight o'clock this morning.
... was sleeping at seven o'clock this morning.
... was reading at nine o'clock last night.
... was watching television at five o'clock yesterday evening.
Example:
Were you speaking English ten minutes ago?
– Yes, I was. / No, I wasn't.

4 Story time

1 Work in pairs. Complete this sentence.
I was walking home last night when I saw ...

2 Give your sentence to another pair.

3 When you receive a sentence, write the next line of the story and give it to another pair.

4 Continue until the story has ten sentences.

5 Read your story to the class.

5 Tune in Book reviews

1 Choose one of these books to read. Give reasons for your choice.

Frantic is a good book for horror addicts. It is about a boy who goes on holiday to Scotland alone. He stays in an old castle and one night he hears strange sounds outside his bedroom door. He decides to investigate and discovers a world of horror.

Secret Codes is a great read for lovers of spy and adventure novels. Pam is a young American diplomat who discovers that some computer disks have disappeared from the American embassy in Berlin. The disks contain information which is vital to American security.

Broken Truce is a western with a difference. It is the story of four brothers who find gold in Arizona - gold which brings trouble with the local people! This book combines intrigue, action and romance - a good read.

2 Listen. Compare the reviews you hear with the three above.

26 p122

6 Language study
Relative pronouns

1 Study these sentences:
1 I read the book that Jonathan gave me.
2 It is about a girl that finds a magic ring.
3 It is a magic ring which allows her to travel through time.
4 But the person who uses the ring grows old very quickly.

2 Copy and complete the table with a tick (✔) or a cross (✗) to find the rule.

	that	who	which
things			
people/things			
people			

7 Book talk

1 Copy and complete these sentences.
I like books which/that ...
I hate books which/that ...
I like heroes/heroines who/that ...
I hate heroes/heroines who/that ...
I like endings which/that ...
I hate endings which/that ...

2 Listen to your partner's sentences and suggest a book for him/her to read.

8 Connections

1 Use the prompts to write your own story.
1 Catherine is a girl (who/which) is (tall/short/intelligent/stupid).
Example:
Catherine is a girl who is tall and intelligent.
2 She is walking in the country when she comes to a river (who/that) is (wide/narrow/slow/fast/safe/dangerous).
3 She sees a bridge (which/who) looks (safe/dangerous).
4 She crosses the bridge and goes into a wood (who/which) is (dark/light).
5 She goes into the wood and meets a person (which/who) is ...
6 Later she finds a box (which/that) contains ...

2 Turn to PAIRWORK A20 p106 to interpret your story.

9 Dictation
Ⓐ Turn to PAIRWORK A21 p106
Ⓑ Turn to PAIRWORK B18 p113

10 Spot check

1 Match the sentence to the correct diagram.
I was talking to a friend when I heard an explosion.

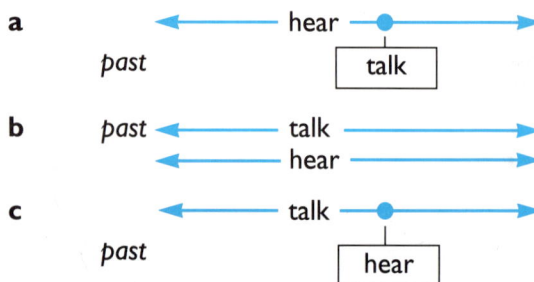

a   hear — talk / past
b   past — talk / hear
c   past — talk — hear

2 Draw your own diagram. Give it to your partner. Your partner writes a sentence about your diagram.

WRITING *Book reviews*

1 Read this review of a book called *Blue Moon*.
1 What kind of book is it?
2 What does the writer think of the book?

2 Answer these questions in pairs.
1 Which paragraph describes the story?
2 What tense does the writer use to describe the story?
3 What does the second paragraph do?

Blue Moon is the story of a Vietnamese girl called Suzi Minh who meets and falls in love with an English boy called Richard. Suzi is on holiday in Europe when she meets Richard. Suzi's parents are very conservative and they do not allow Suzi to see Richard. Suzi and Richard run away to France, but Suzi's brothers find them and try to take her back to her family. Richard fights them, but one of the brothers shoots him and he dies. Suzi returns to her family.

Blue Moon is a very sad story, but it is beautifully written. I recommend this book to anyone who likes romantic novels.

3 Where do these extracts come from in the book?
a beginning
b middle
c end

1 They were walking along the road in the rain when a police car stopped in front of them.
A policeman got out to talk to them.
'Passeports, s'il vous plaît.'
Richard looked at Suzi. He did not understand.

2 Suzi was crying when she got on the plane.

3 Suzi was dreaming of her holiday in Europe when her father came in.
'We've got the tickets, Suzi. We leave next week.'
They both smiled.

4 Use the notes to write a book review.

5 Write a sentence from the beginning, middle and end of the book *Eagle Peak*.

6 Write a review of a book you have read recently.

7 Read the reviews other students wrote. Choose a book to read.

EAGLE PEAK

two friends (Simon and Jo) /go climbing/
Rocky mountains /Jo break leg/
Simon get help /helicopter rescue/
not very good /boring /not recommend

UNIT 14 On the road

1 WESTGATE KIDS
EPISODE 6

1 Read the story. Why is Matt talking to Mike?

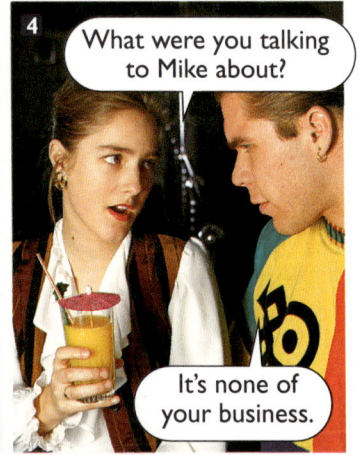

I'm sorry dad, but …

Don't worry.

At the police station

Later that evening

You'd better keep quiet!

Why is Matt talking to Mike?

What were you talking to Mike about?

It's none of your business.

Come on. Let's go!

But we've just arrived.

I don't care.

He's acting really strangely.

Let's take a taxi.

I've only had one drink!

But we might have an accident.

Stop moaning and get on!

Look out!

SHOEI

2 🔲 Listen. Did Mike recognise the person who broke into the school?

➤➤➤ 27 p122

64

2 Language study
will and *might*

1 Study this:

will ✔✔	might ✔ ?
will not (won't) ✗✗	might not (mightn't) ✗ ?

2 What is the difference in meaning between *will* and *might*?

3 Copy and complete these sentences (from Activity 1, tapescript) with the correct symbols from the diagram above (✔✔, ✗✗, ✔?, or ✗ ?).
1 I ____ tell the police. I'm not sure.
2 ____ you come home with me now?
3 I ____ be so hard in the future.
4 I ____ try to work harder.
5 I ____ pass all my exams.
6 We ____ worry about that when it happens.

4 Match the sentences to the speakers.

| Mike | Mike's dad |

5 📼 Listen to check.

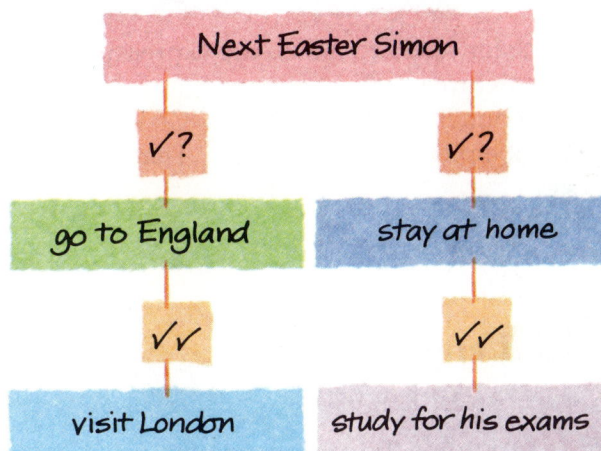

3 If ...

1 Look at the diagrams and write two or three sentences for each one. The first one has been done for you.

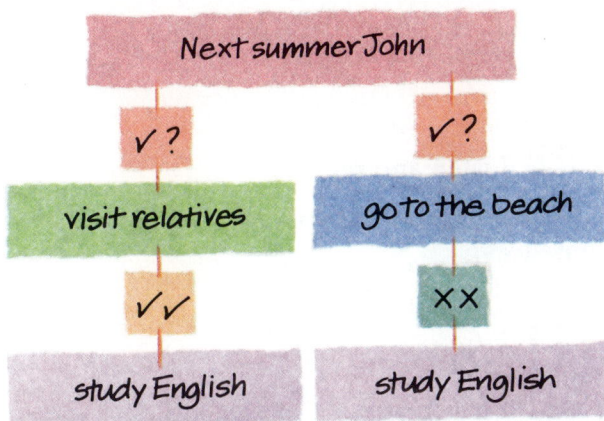

Next summer John
✔ ?
visit relatives
✔ ✔
study English

go to the beach
✗ ✗
study English

Example:
Next summer, John might visit his relatives, or he might go to the beach. If he visits his relatives, he will study English. If he goes to the beach, he won't.

Next Christmas Sarah
✔?
go on holiday
✗ ✗
get a lot of presents

✔?
stay at home
✔ ✔
get a lot of presents

Next Easter Simon
✔?
go to England
✔ ✔
visit London

✔?
stay at home
✔ ✔
study for his exams

2 Choose two of the following and make diagrams about yourself.
1 next summer
2 next Christmas
3 next Easter

3 Exchange diagrams with your partner and write two sentences for each one.

4 Game When I am 30

1 Work in groups of four. Copy the table and write the names of the three other students.

	you		
be famous			
be rich			
get married			
be a doctor			
live in Great Britain			

2 Complete the table for yourself with ✔✔, ✗✗, ✔?, or ✗ ?. Then ask questions to complete the table for the other students. Guess what their answers will be.

3 You score five points for each correct guess.

5 Tune in Scenes

1 📼 **Listen and match the conversations to a picture.**

2 Listen again to match the expressions to the pictures.

Well done!   Hang on!   Good luck!
What a pity!   Don't worry.   That's great!

≫≫ 28 p122

6 Language study

Everyday English

1 Complete the exchanges with a suitable expression.
1 I've passed my exam!   a ____
2 Are you ready yet?   b ____
3 I've lost my favourite earring.   c ____
4 My driving test is tomorrow.   d ____
5 I'm sorry I forgot your birthday.   e ____

2 📼 **Listen to check.**

3 How do you translate the expressions into your language?

7 Good news

1 Work in pairs. Write a short dialogue for the story. Use everyday English.

2 Act out your dialogue for another pair.

8 Game What a pity!

1 Work in groups. Write these expressions on pieces of paper to make expression cards.
Well done!   That's great!
What a pity!   Good luck!
Don't worry.

2 Write a piece of good news or bad news.
Example:
I have just passed my exams.

3 In turns, read your news to the others.

4 When you hear the news, put a suitable exression card on the table.

5 You win two points each time you put the most suitable expression card on the table.
Example:
I have just passed my exams. /Well done!

9 Sounds right

1 Match the stress patterns to these sentences.
1 What will you do if you pass your exams?
2 I will go to university.
3 Will you go to that concert next week?
4 I might.
5 Will you go to the beach next summer?
6 Yes, I will.

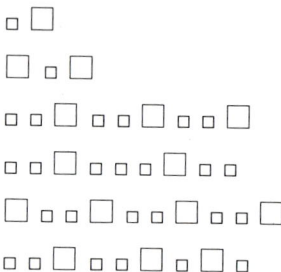

□ □
□ □ □
□□ □ □□ □ □□ □
□□ □ □□□ □□□
□ □□ □□ □ □□ □
□□ □ □□ □ □ □

2 📼 **Listen and repeat.**

3 Which patterns do you hear in the next five sentences?

10 Spot check

1 Work in groups. Use these words to write four sentences about your life.
will   will not   might   might not

2 What did the other students in your group write?

Road safety

1 READING
A poster

Read the poster. Find appropriate pieces of advice to match to the pictures.

WATCH OUT!

▲ **Wear it!** Helmets are essential if you have a motorbike.

▲ **Put it on!** Safety belts in cars greatly reduce your chances of major injury in an accident.

▲ **Stop!** Never drink and drive.

▲ **Look out!** Always look in your mirror before overtaking.

▲ **Slow down!** Respect the speed limits.

▲ **Take a break!** If you are tired, leave your car or motorbike and take public transport.

▲ **Don't gamble!** Never drive through a red traffic light.

2 LISTENING
Speeds

1 [cassette] **Match the words to the pictures.** road

street   A road   B road
motorway

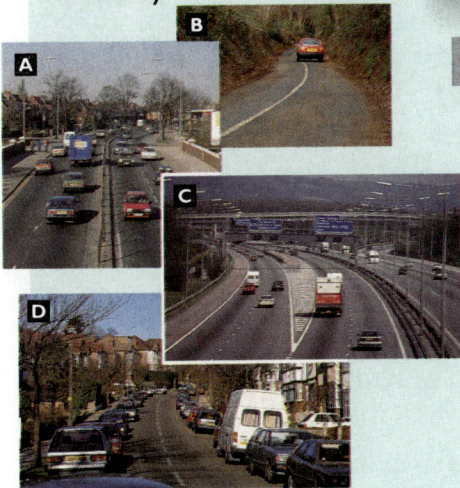

2 How many kilometres are there to one mile?
a 2 km   b 1.53 km   c 1.60 km

2 How many kilometres are there to one mile?
a 2 km   b 1.53 km   c 1.60 km

3 VOCABULARY *Picture dictionary*

1 **Match the words to the pictures.**
Transport
traffic lights   road sign   zebra crossing   roundabout

2 **Write another word you associate with transport. Find a picture for it.**

3 **Find some words and pictures for these headings.**
a films   b sport

4 FOLLOW UP

Make a road saftey poster to display in class.

Review and Extension 4

1 Grammar

■ Past continuous

1 Work in pairs. Use the prompts to write what happened to Sandra yesterday.
Example:
She was having a shower when the phone rang.
a eat breakfast/postman deliver letters
b drive car/tyre burst
c do shopping/meet Julie
d wait in queue/man take her purse

2 What were you doing at these times yesterday?
1 nine o'clock in the morning
2 midday
3 two o'clock in the afternoon
4 eight o'clock in the evening

3 Ask your partner and write sentences.

■ Relative pronouns

1 Work in pairs. Do the quiz as quickly as possible.
1 Name a book that ends happily.
2 Name a film that ends sadly.
3 Name a person in the class who has been abroad.
4 Name a city which has a university.
5 Name a country which is surrounded by sea.
6 Name a person who has won two Olympic gold medals.

2 Make your own 'Name a ...' quiz for another pair.

■ *will* and *might*

1 Guess what three other students will or will not do this weekend. Write three sentences.
Example:
I think Maria will watch television.

2 Read your sentences to the three students. Were your guesses correct?
Example:
Maria, will you watch television this weekend?

2 Vocabulary

1 Look at the picture. Copy and complete the description with these words.
next to   on   in front of   in   over   under

John has a large room. 1 ____ the wall by his bed is a poster of Michael Jackson and 2 ____ his bed is a small table with a light on it. 3 ____ the window is a desk. Hanging from the ceiling 4 ____ the desk is a model aeroplane. 5 _____ the desk is a wastepaper basket. John keeps his clothes 6 ____ the wardrobe.

2 Write a description of your bedroom. Give it to another student to draw.

3 In conversation

1 Work in pairs. Say these expressions in your language.

1. What were you doing when the doorbell rang?
2. When did you get here?
3. Where were you while she was speaking?
4. What'll happen tomorrow?
5. I might try to escape.

2 You are in prison with a friend. Use three of these expressions in a dialogue.

3 Act out your dialogue for another pair.

4 Study skills Assessing progress

1 Write a list of ten items you have studied this term.
Example:
● *the first conditional*   ● *food vocabulary*

2 Order the things from 1 to 10 (1 = very confident about, 10 = not very confident about). Compare your list with that of another student.

The Guardians
EPISODE 4

1 The adventure diary

1 Copy and complete the diary with the simple past or past continuous form of the verbs in brackets.

Day 7
We (1 wake up) suddenly. A strange figure (2 watch) us from the edge of the clearing. It (3 wear) a white robe which (4 shine) brightly. It (5 raise) its arm and two more figures (6 come) into the clearing. They (7 smile). They (8 give) us food and water and we (9 feel) better immediately. We (10 thank) them. Then the first figure (11 speak) in a magical voice.

2 Voices

Listen to answer the questions.
1 Who is the strange figure?
2 What does he/she want?
3 What does he/she say about the city?

3 Investigate

Rich world, poor world

Turn to Investigation file 4 p118

69

Adventure

UNIT 15

1 Missouri Joan

1 Unjumble the pictures to find the story.

MORE ADVENTURES OF MISSOURI JOAN

In this episode, Joan travels to Egypt to find the lost tomb of a Pharaoh.

A

Aagh!

She fell suddenly.

She screamed.

B

Phew!

She grabbed a rock.

C

The snakes hissed loudly below.

D

I've only got one chance.

She jumped inside quickly.

E

What was that?

Something hit her in the face.

F

She quietly took a torch from her backpack.

G

This is it! The secret door!

The door opened slowly.

2 What do you think will happen next?

1 She will use her rope to climb out.
2 She will find a secret passageway.
3 She will find a secret door and use her knife to open it.
4 She will fall into the pit and the snakes will kill her.

3 🔊 **Listen to check.**

➤➤➤ 29 p122

70

2 Language study Adverbs

1 Study this:
She jumped inside <u>quickly</u>.
The door opened <u>slowly</u>.

2 Do the underlined words describe
a) a noun or b) an action?

3 Match the words to the pictures.
quickly slowly quietly loudly

A

B

C

D

4 Write a sentence for each picture.

5 Study this:
The house was quiet. Everyone was in bed.
'How is she?' he asked quietly.
1 What kind of word is *quiet*?
2 What do we add to *quiet* to make an adverb?

3 Guess what

1 Work in groups. Copy and complete the table. Describe how you and two other students in your group do these things.

	me		
walk			
talk			
eat			
work			
write			

2 Check with the other students.
Example:
I think you write slowly.
– Yes, I do. / No, I don't. I write quickly.

4 Game Mime

1 Work in groups. Write ten verbs and five adverbs on separate pieces of paper.
Example:

verbs	adverbs
eat	happily
dance	slowly

2 In turns, pick up a verb and an adverb and mime the action.

3 Guess what and how the other student is miming.
Example:
I think you are eating slowly.
– Yes, I am. / No, I'm not.

5 Tune in The tomb

1 Unjumble these extracts from the next part of Missouri Joan's adventure.

> She remembered that she had a knife with a saw for cutting wood. She began to cut the wood and after a few minutes there was a loud noise and the rock moved.

> But at the end of the tunnel, an enormous rock blocked the way.

> She pushed the rock to see if it moved, but it was too heavy.

> Joan jumped quickly through the gap. The rock suddenly fell loudly back into place - then all was silent.

> Suddenly, Joan felt a breeze on her face. She began to walk towards it, slowly at first and then more quickly, hoping to find the way out.

> She was free, but where was the gold?

> Then she noticed a small space at the side of the rock with a piece of wood in it.

2 Listen to check.

30 p122

6 Language study

Talking about purpose

1 Find the meaning of the underlined words.
1 She pushed the rock <u>to see if it moved</u>.
   Meaning: a why she pushed the rock.
              b how she pushed the rock.
2 The knife had a small saw <u>for cutting wood</u>.
   Meaning: a why the saw was small.
              b what the saw was used for.

2 Complete the sentences.
1 I go to school to ...
2 My school bag is full of things for ...
3 My teacher gives us homework to ...
4 Holidays are for ...

3 Ask questions to find out what your partner wrote.
Example:
Why do you go to school?
What are the things in your school bag for?

7 An adventurer's backpack

1 Work in pairs. You are going on a journey into the desert.

2 Choose six of these objects to take with you. Say why you want to take each one.
a tent   two blankets   two bottles   a compass
a knife   soap   matches   a mirror   a rope
a book   a radio   a gun
Example:
A: *I think we should take a tent.*
B: *Why?*
A: *To sleep in.*

8 Lateral thinking

1 Work in pairs. How many different uses can you think of for a brick?
Example:
for keeping the door open / for weightlifting

2 Ask another pair to think of uses for a different object.
Example: *a safety pin*

9 Sounds right

1 Mark the stress in these words.
silent   quickly   desperate   loudly   loud
angrily   desperately   silently   angry   quick
Example:

□ □
silent

2 Listen to check.

10 Spot check

1 Copy and complete the rule.
We form regular adverbs by adding __ to the __.

2 Make adverbs from the following adjectives.
a angry   c beautiful
b happy   d dangerous

3 Complete the sentences with an appropriate adverb.
1 The children were laughing and playing ____ together at the party.
2 It was a brilliant performance. He sang ____.
3 She was driving very ____ along the mountain road. She almost had an accident.
4 The two men shouted ____ at each other.

ASSIGNMENT 9
Games

1 READING *Game*

Work in groups. Read the rules to play
The Map game.

RULES
- Play the game in groups of four. There are two teams – two players in each team.
- Write each of these verbs on small paper squares (☐).
  run smile speak eat
  stand up open jump
- Write each of these adverbs on small paper triangles (△).
  slowly angrily loudly desperately
  quickly beautifully dangerously
- Place the pieces of paper face down on the table - verbs on the right and adverbs on the left. In turns, one player from each pair picks up one of the verbs and one of the adverbs.
- He/she mimes the action for his/her partner. Example: *sing beautifully*
- If you guess correctly what your partner is miming, you move one space towards the treasure. If you do not guess correctly, you move two spaces back.

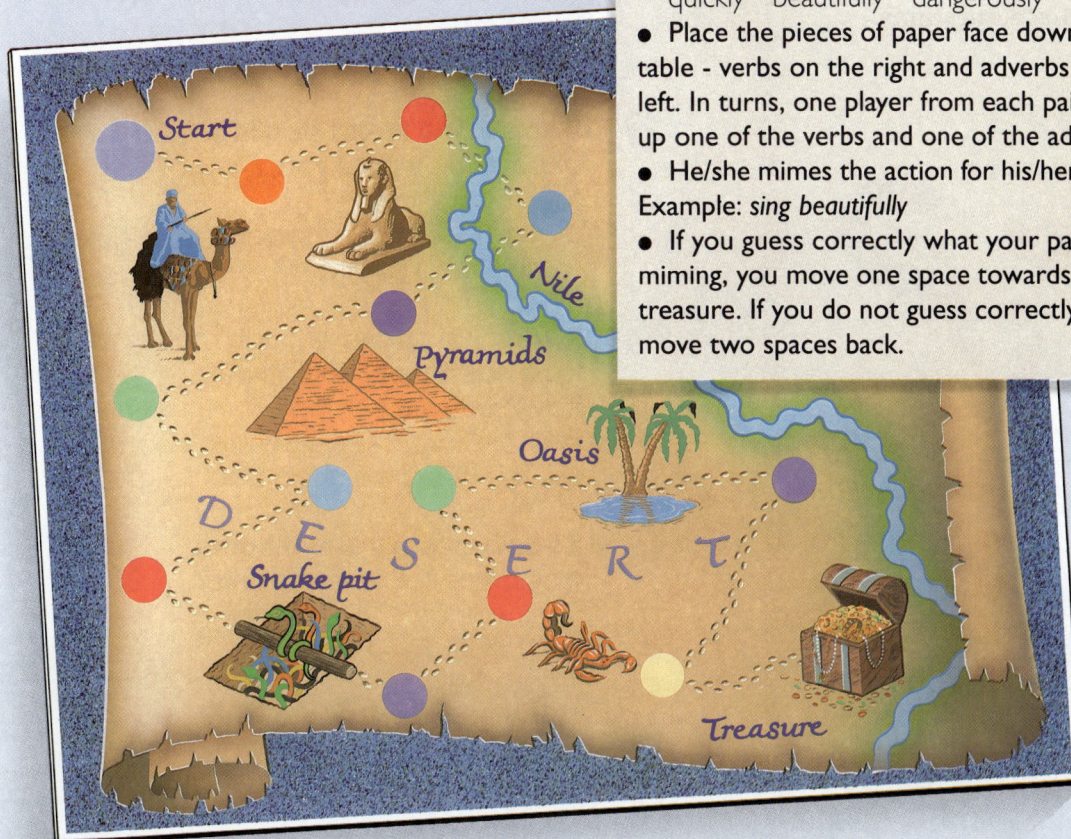

2 LISTENING
Shapes and sizes

1 **Match these words to the picture.**
circle triangle square rectangle

2 🔊 **Listen. Follow the instructions.**

3 **Draw a pattern on a piece of paper and dictate your pattern to your partner.**
Example:

3 VOCABULARY
Word games

1 **Choose a game and find out how to play it.**
Twenty questions (PAIRWORK A22 p106)
One minute! (PAIRWORK B19 p113)

2 **Describe how to play the game to another student.**

3 **Play the game.**

4 FOLLOW UP

Make a game to practise English.

Personality

1 Honesty

1 Answer these questions.

How honest are you?

1 **If you saw £5 in the street, would you ...**
a pick it up and keep it?
b leave it?
c give it to charity?

2 **If you saw a friend stealing chocolate, would you ...**
a take no notice?
b tell him/her to put it back?
c tell the shop assistant?

3 **If you didn't have enough money for a bus ticket, would you ...**
a travel without paying?
b walk?
c ask the bus driver for a free ticket?

4 **If you broke a vase at home, would you tell your parents?**
a No, I wouldn't.
b Yes, I would.
c It depends.

5 **Would you take a day off school for no reason?**
a Yes, I would.
b No, I wouldn't.
c It depends.

6 **If you forgot to do your homework, would you ...**
a tell your teacher you were ill?
b tell your teacher the truth?
c copy your friend's homework?

7 **Do you copy in exams?**
a Always.
b Never.
c Sometimes.

8 **Have you ever told a lie?**
a Hundreds of times.
b Never.
c Once or twice.

2 Interview your partner. Who is more honest: you or your partner?

Score

If all your answers are **a** you are not very honest.

If all your answers are **b** you are very honest.

If all your answers are **c** you try to be honest.

2 Language study
Second conditional

1 Study this sentence.

improbable condition	+	improbable result
If I saw £5 in the street,		I would keep it.

2

improbable condition	+	improbable result
If + _____ ,		_____ + infinitive without *to*.

3 🔊 **Listen. Copy and complete the sentences.**

1 If there _____ nobody looking, I _____ _____ it in my pocket.

2 If I _____ a friend stealing chocolate, I _____ _____ _____ the shop assistant.

3 I _____ _____ _____ a very good friend if I _____ the shop assistant.

» 31 p122

3 Dilemmas

Work in pairs. What would you do if you found:

1 a fly in your soup in a restaurant.

2 a love letter from your best friend to your boy/girlfriend.

3 your birthday present from your mum and dad two days before your birthday, and you really disliked it.

4 the answers for the end of year exam at school.

5 a photograph of your teacher in fancy dress.

Example:

If I found a fly in my soup, I would not eat it.

4 Game Shipwrecked

1 Work in pairs. Look at the picture. Copy and complete the sentence.

If I weren't on this island, I would _____ and I wouldn't _____.

2 Use the pictures to write three more sentences.

3 You are shipwrecked on a desert island. Think of five things you would/would not do if you left the island. Write five questions to interview your partner.

Example:

If you weren't on a desert island, would you study English? - Yes, I would./No, I wouldn't.

4 Do you and your partner agree about what you would do? If you agree, then you can escape.

5 Tune in Rick's problem

1 📼 **Listen. What is Rick's problem?**

2 Listen again. What advice does Tom give Rick?
1 see a doctor
2 invite Tracy to the cinema
3 go to a disco
4 organise a party

3 What other advice does Tom give?

»32 p122

6 Language study
Giving advice (2)

1 Which words does Tom use to give advice? Copy and complete the word spider.

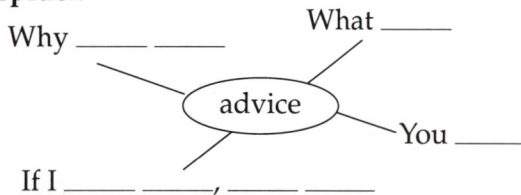

Why _____   What _____

advice

You _____

If I _____ , _____

2 Work in pairs. You give these pieces of advice to five different people. What is each person's problem?
1 If I were you, I'd find a part time job.
2 Why don't you tell them you can't?
3 What about sending some flowers?
4 You should talk to your teacher.
5 If I were you, I wouldn't see him any more.

3 Compare your work with that of another pair. Who thought of the most interesting problems?

7 Game The little devil

Work in groups of three.
A Turn to PAIRWORK A23 p106
B Turn to PAIRWORK B20 p113
C Turn to PAIRWORK A32 p108

8 Types of people

1 Match the words to a dictionary definition.

shy
cheerful
aggressive
nervous
energetic

1 (adj) apprehensive, worried

2 (adj) timid, uneasy with other people

3 (adj) happy, light-hearted

4 (adj) hostile, belligerent

5 (adj) enthusiastic, determined

2 📼 **Listen to the five teenagers. What type of people are they?**
shy cheerful aggressive nervous energetic

3 Write a piece of advice for each of them.

9 Dictation
A Turn to PAIRWORK A24 p107
B Turn to PAIRWORK B21 p113

10 Spot check

1 Work in pairs. Copy and complete these sentences.
1 If I were a famous person, I would be …
2 I would eat raw eggs if …
3 If I were the teacher, I would …
4 If I ruled the world, I would …

2 Compare your work with that of another pair. Who wrote the most interesting sentences?

WRITING *Descriptions*

1 Read the descriptions and choose the best adjectives to describe each teenager.
serious caring loyal helpful understanding fun generous

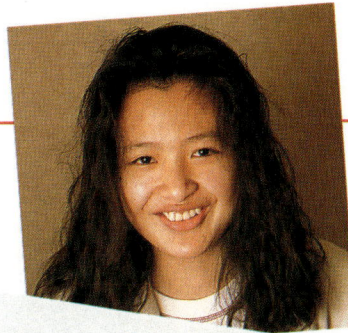

Barbara never criticises her friends and she is a good listener. She is great to talk to if you have a problem. She is also very generous. If you wanted to borrow something, she would lend it to you. She is a relaxed person and enjoys a good joke.

Heinz is a very intelligent, gentle person. He is interested in the environment. He likes to spend his free time playing chess, reading or talking to friends. He is a member of Greenpeace and the World Wide Fund. He doesn't really like sport.

Pablo is the type of friend who would help you if you had a problem. He never talks about his friends behind their backs. If you have a secret you can trust him to keep it for you.

Joan really likes having a good time. She enjoys listening to music, dancing and going to discos. She always knows what to do and where to go at the weekend. She is very fashionable. Her parents own a boutique and she always wears fantastic outfits. Sometimes she is not a very loyal friend.

2 Choose one of the teenagers to be your friend.

3 Tell your partner who you chose and why. Start like this:
I chose X because ...

4 Look at the scale Pablo made. Who is his best friend: Barbara, Heinz or Joan?

5 In pairs, make a scale showing what you value in a good friend.

6 Which qualities were the most/least important for another pair?

7 Describe your best friend to your partner.
Example:
My best friend is a lot of fun. He/She likes listening to music.

8 Write descriptions of three of your friends.

My friend should...

10 — be loyal
9 — be easy-going
8 — have the same interests as me
7 — have a sense of humour
6 — be intelligent
5 — like the same music as me
4 — be good-looking
3 — like nice clothes
2 — have a fashionable hairstyle
1 — be rich

Scenes

1 WESTGATE KIDS
EPISODE 7

1 How long have I been here?

Since last night.

2 He's really nice.

She's beautiful.

Is it OK if I visit tomorrow?

Yes, of course.

3 Susan, are you all right?

Yes, Mum. Don't worry.

4 Where's Susan?

Just leave her alone. She doesn't need you!

5 It's over!

But Susan ...

Match these phrases to the scenes. Listen to check.
- Right, I'll go now.
- It was a mistake.
- You've been sleeping for six hours.
- Bye.
- What happened?
- I don't want to see you any more.

33 p122

78

2 Language study

Present perfect simple/present perfect continuous

1 **Study these sentences.**
1 I have known my teacher for two years.
2 I have been studying English for two years.

2 **Which tense is used in each sentence?**

3 **How is the verb form made in each sentence?**

4 **Which sentence describes an activity and which describes a state?**

5 **Use the prompts to write sentences about the illustrations.**

a run/two hours

b study Japanese/three years

c be a teacher/five years

d know best friend/six months

3 For or since

1 **Match the two parts of the sentences.**
1 I have been here for   ... ten o'clock.
2 I have been here since   ... two hours.
3 I have known him for   ... June.
4 I have known him since   ... a month.

2 **Choose the correct statement.**
1 We use *for*:
a when we give the starting point of the action.
b when we describe how long the action has lasted.
2 We use *since*:
a when we give the starting point of the action.
b when we describe how long the action has lasted.

3 **Complete these sentences with information about yourself.**
1 I have been studying English for ...
2 I have known my best friend since ...
3 I have lived in my house/flat for ...

4 **In pairs, ask and answer questions.**
Example:
How long have you been studying English for?
- I have been studying English for a year.

4 Game How long for?

1 **Work in pairs. Write four things your partner is wearing.**

2 **In turns, guess how long he/she has had those clothes for.**
Example:
I think you have had your jeans for six months.
- Yes, I have./ No, I haven't.

Scoring
50 points exact time
30 points within one month
10 points within two months

3 **Write four true sentences about your partner's clothes using *since*.**
Example:
My partner has had his/her jeans since June.

5 Tune in

1 📼 **Listen. What two things does Susan want to do?**

Susan is out of hospital.

2 Work in pairs.

👥 **A** Turn to PAIRWORK A25 p107
B Turn to PAIRWORK B22 p113

➤➤ (34) p122

6 Language study

Asking for and giving permission

1 Look at the pictures. Use the prompts to complete the dialogues.

1
A: Can I ...?
B: Yes, sure.
2
A: Is it OK if I ...?
B: Yes, of course.
3
A: Could I ...?
B: No, I'm sorry but ...

2 Write four lines to continue one of the dialogues.
Example:
A: *Can I borrow your bicycle?*
B: *Yes, sure.*
A: *Thanks. I'll bring it back tomorrow.*
B: *Oh, but I need it tonight.*
A: *Is it OK if I bring it back at eight?*
B: *No, I'm sorry. I need it at seven.*

7 Pairwork

👥 **A** Turn to PAIRWORK A26 p107
B Turn to PAIRWORK B23 p113

8 Survey Permission

1 Do you have permission to do these things?
- use the telephone as often as you want
- stay up late
- go to discos alone
- stay at a friend's house
- stay out late at night

2 Interview three other students. Who has permission to do all of these things?

9 Sounds right

1 📼 **Listen to these sounds.**
1 /v/ 2 /b/

2 How many times do you hear each sound in the sentences? Copy and complete the table.

	/v/	/b/
1	3	2
2		
3		
4		
5		

3 Write two sentences of your own. Include the sounds /v/ and /b/. Read the sentences to your partner. Ask him/her how many times the sounds appear in each sentence.

10 Spot check

1 Copy the word spiders. Match the correct expressions to each.
four years   last Wednesday   a week
six months   6 June 1993   ten days
a long time   May

for   since

2 Use the present perfect simple and the present perfect continuous to write two sentences with *since* and two with *for*.

Mistakes

1 READING
Correcting

1 Work in pairs. Match the correction symbols to the words.

Ww	Wrong tense
Wp	Too many words
X	Wrong word order
Sp	Wrong word
Wt	Wrong punctuation
Wo	Spelling

2 Use the symbols and the words underlined to rewrite the essay correctly.

3 Compare your work with that of another pair.

4 Write your own version of _Parents_.

5 Give your version to another pair to check.

2 LISTENING
Opinions

1 📟 **Work in pairs. Listen to a teacher talking about learning a language. Tick (✓) the points she mentions.**

1	Do your homework.
2	Do not speak Spanish in class.
3	Learn a lot of grammar.
4	Try to communicate in English from the first moment.
5	Do not worry about making mistakes when you write.
6	Try to say everything perfectly.
7	Learn from your mistakes.

2 What two other pieces of advice does she give?

Parents

Sp Wp My parents are quiet strict, during
X X   the week I can not to go out at all.
  X   I have to be come straight home after
  X   school. I can to watch television for
       half an hour in the evening, but only
       after I have done my homework. On
Sp   satudays I can go out with my friends.
Wt   We are usually going to a disco or a
Wt Ww coffee bar. I go to discos since two
Wo   years. I get always home before
Wp   eleven o'clock. If not there is
       big trouble!

---

3 VOCABULARY _False friends_

1 Match the words to a definition.

pregnant
relative
parent
embarrassed

1 ____ (adj) to be shocked by something. To feel nervous, uncomfortable or ashamed.
2 ____ (adj) to be expecting a baby
3 ____ (n) your mother or father
4 ____ (n) a member of your family

2 Copy and complete the sentences with these words.

pregnant   parents   embarrassed   relatives

1 I am really ____. I called her Lucy all evening and then I found out her name was Michelle.
2 All John's ____ live in Oxford, so it will be easy for them to come to the wedding.
3 Her ____ have gone to the school to speak to the teachers about her progress.
4 She is eight months ____ now. The baby is due in May.

4 FOLLOW UP

1 Work in pairs. Unjumble the words to find two false friends and match them to a definition.

a CLUATA   b RSEPNET

1 ____ (adj) real, certain, undeniable
2 ____ (adj) at the moment, now

2 Write a sentence with each word.

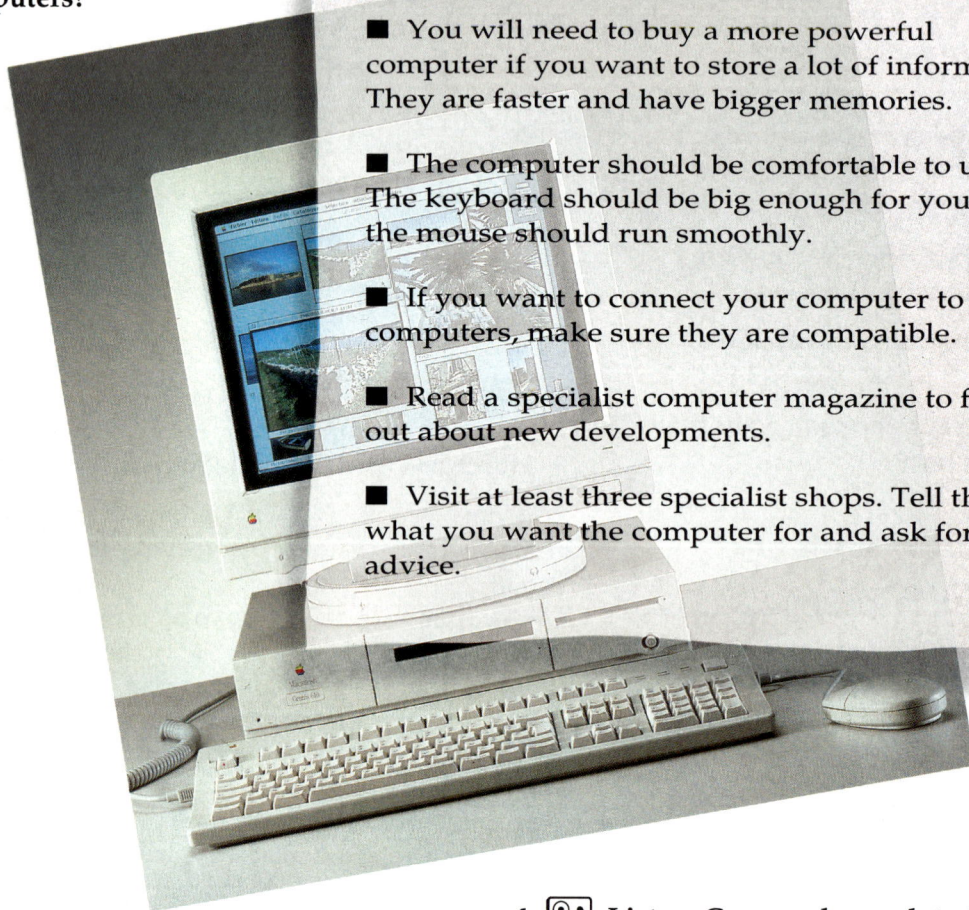

Technology

1 Computers

1 Which words would you expect to find in an article about computers?

program
memory
dress
monitor
lens
powerful
hard disk
mouse
compatible
table
cat
floppy disk
keyboard

STAR TIPS *Choosing a computer*

■ Firstly, decide what you want the computer for: games, letters or calculations.

■ If you only want the computer for games, do not buy an expensive one. However, you will need a colour monitor.

■ You will need to buy a more powerful computer if you want to store a lot of information. They are faster and have bigger memories.

■ The computer should be comfortable to use. The keyboard should be big enough for you and the mouse should run smoothly.

■ If you want to connect your computer to other computers, make sure they are compatible.

■ Read a specialist computer magazine to find out about new developments.

■ Visit at least three specialist shops. Tell them what you want the computer for and ask for their advice.

2 Look at the text quickly. How many of the words can you find?

3 Answer these questions.
1 What three uses of a computer are mentioned?
2 What type of computer do you need if you want to play games?
3 What two advantages do more powerful computers have?
4 What two aspects of comfort are mentioned in the text?
5 Why should you visit three computer shops?

4 ▣ Listen. Copy and complete the table.

	AGM 24	AGM 28
cheaper		
more powerful		
bigger colour monitor		
clearer colour monitor		
faster		
bigger keyboard		

5 Which star tips from the text do the salesman and the customer follow?

》》》 35 p122

2 Language study *as ... as*

1 Match the sentences that have the same meaning.

AX1

AX2

AX3

1 The AX1 is as big as the AX2.
2 The AX2 is not as big as the AX3.
3 The AX3 is not as small as the AX2.
a The AX2 is smaller than the AX3.
b The AX1 and the AX2 are the same size.
c The AX3 is bigger than the AX2.

2 Read the sentences.
1 The FAB is cheaper than the PLC.
2 The Power is more expensive than the PLC.
3 The Power is not as expensive as the ALS.
4 The Quadrant is the most expensive.

3 Copy and complete the table with the appropriate prices.

£500 £1,500 £3,000 £750 £2,500

Computer	Price
FAB	
PLC	
Power	
ALS	
Quadrant	

3 Computer games

1 Compare the computer games with these adjectives. You have five minutes to write as many sentences as you can.

expensive cheap interesting boring
Example:
Air Battle is not as interesting as Lost in Space.

2 Compare your sentences with your partner's.

3 Compare two computer or video games you know.

4 Pairwork Puzzle it out

A Turn to PAIRWORK A27 p107
B Turn to PAIRWORK B24 p113

5 Tune in Revolution at work

1 Copy and complete the text with these words.

handle large messages typewriters
operator telephone

At the beginning of the century people used to send 1 _____ by telegraph and only a few people had telephones. To make a 2 _____ call, you used to turn a 3 _____ and wait for the 4 _____ to answer.

The first 5 _____ were large and heavy, and some of the computers developed after World War II were so 6 _____ that they used to fill a whole room. They were also very slow.

2 🔊 **Listen to check.**

▶▶▶ 36 p122

6 Language study *used to*

1 Study these sentences.
What does *used to* mean?
1 People used to send messages by telegraph, but they do not now.
2 People did not use to have telephones, but they do now.

2 Look at the picture. Write five sentences explaining what people used to or did not use to do.
Example:
People did not use to travel by car.
They used to travel by horse.

7 A long time ago

👥 🅰 Turn to PAIRWORK A28 p107
🅱 Turn to PAIRWORK B25 p114

8 The good old days

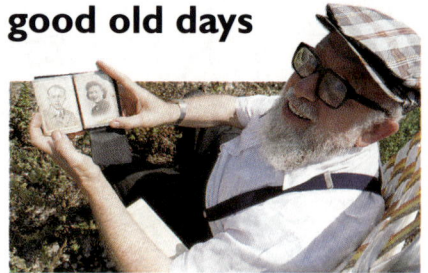

1 Do you think the man in the picture will say these things?
1 Life used to be slower when I was a boy.
2 People used to travel a lot to different countries.
3 People used to work with computers.
4 People used to have more time to talk.

2 🔊 **Listen to check.**

3 Use the prompts to write questions to ask the speaker.
Example:
life/be/slower/when you/be/a boy?
Did life use to be slower when you were a boy?
1 people/travel/a lot/different countries?
2 people/work/with computers?
3 people/have/more time to talk?

4 In pairs, act out the interview.

5 Tell your partner about two things you used to or did not use to do when you were younger.

9 Dictation

👥 🅰 Turn to PAIRWORK A29 p107
🅱 Turn to PAIRWORK B26 p114

10 Spot check

1 Rewrite these sentences so that the information is correct.
1 Paris is not as big as Madrid.
2 Computers used to be very small.
3 Calculators are as expensive as portable computers.
4 At the beginning of the century people did not use to travel by train.

2 Write four more incorrect sentences with *used to* and *as ... as*. Give them to your partner to correct.

WRITING *History*

Saturn

1 Answer the questions in this space quiz.

1 When was the first satellite launched?
  a 1925   b 1957   c 1980

2 Who launched the first satellite?
  a USA   b USSR   c France

3 Who was the first man in space?
  a Scott   b Gagarin   c Armstrong

4 Who was the first man on the moon?
  a Gagarin   b Columbus   c Armstrong

5 When did the first man walk on the moon?
  a 1955   b 1969   c 1970

6 Which probe reached Saturn in 1979?
  a Pioneer 11   b Voyager 2   c Challenger

2 Read the text to check.

Yuri Gagarin

Voyager 2

Neil Armstrong

THE SPACE AGE

In 1957, the USSR launched the first satellite into space and the space age began. In 1961, the USSR sent the first man into space. His name was Yuri Gagarin and he was only 26 years old.

In 1969 the first person, Neil Armstrong an American astronaut, walked on the moon. This was one of the most dramatic events in the history of mankind.

Both the USSR and the USA have sent space probes to every planet. Pioneer 11 reached Saturn in 1979, while Voyager 2 reached Uranus in 1986 and sent back photographs of Neptune in 1989.

3 Use the prompts to write a paragraph about how people used to live in the age of steam.
a 1750 Industrial Revolution starts
b 1764 Watt develops efficient steam engine
c people leave the countryside to work in factories in the towns
d children work in the mines
e people travel by horse and carriage
f steam trains transport goods
g people travel across the sea by steamship

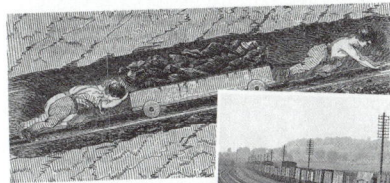

4 Choose one of these periods of history. Find out about it and write a paragraph.
1 Stone Age
2 Iron Age
3 Middle Ages

Review and Extension 5

1 Grammar

■ Second conditional

1 Complete these sentences.
1 If I had three wishes, ...
2 If I ruled the world, ...
3 If I were the headmaster/headmistress, ...
4 The world would be a better place if ...

2 Which person in the class has the best endings for each sentence?

■ *as ... as*

Find someone who ...
... is not as tall as you.
... has a brother who is as old as you.
... has as much money as you in his/her pocket.
... is as intelligent as you.
... is as good at English as you.
... has feet as big as yours.

■ *used to*

1 Write a sentence for each topic about how your tastes have changed.
Example:
food- *I used to like eating chocolate, but now I do not.*
1 food
2 clothes
3 music
4 entertainment

2 Guess what your partner wrote. Were you right?

2 Vocabulary

1 Copy the sentences and tick (✔) the ones that are true for you.
1 I run more quickly than my friend.
2 I talk louder than my mum.
3 I eat more slowly than my dad.
4 I climb trees more easily than a monkey.
5 I speak English better than my little brother.

2 Write four sentences with adverbs about your partner.
Example:
Mark runs more quickly than Tony.

3 Tell your partner your sentences. Does he/she agree?

3 In conversation

1 Work in pairs. Say these expressions in your language.

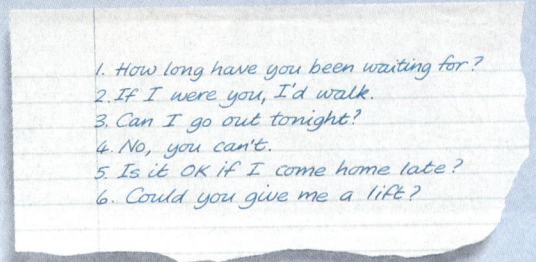

1. How long have you been waiting for?
2. If I were you, I'd walk.
3. Can I go out tonight?
4. No, you can't.
5. Is it OK if I come home late?
6. Could you give me a lift?

2 You are out cycling and meet your mum standing at the bus stop. Use four of these expressions in a dialogue.

3 Act out your dialogue for another pair.

4 Study skills English around you

1 Look at the picture. Make a list of the resources you have to learn English.

2 Where can you find these resources in your town? Make a list of places and find out the addresses. What can you find there?
Example:
library - dictionaries

3 Display the information as a poster.

The Guardians
EPISODE 5

1 The adventure diary

1 Complete the diary with these words.

have given   found
have reached   has brought
wants   is sitting
have been following

Day 8
Exhausted! We [1] _____ the Guardians
for a day without stopping...
Day 9
'We [2] _____ the Guardians' city. It is
fantastic. It is full of flowers and
gardens. The Guardians are very friendly
and they [3] _____ us more of their
delicious food. We feel great!
Day 10
The man who [4] _____ us in the
clearing [5] _____ us to a large
building in the centre of the city.
Inside it is dark and a very old
man [6] _____ in the darkness. He
[7] _____ to talk to us.

2 Voices

Listen.
1 Who is the old man?
2 What is his message?
3 Why is the message important?

3 Investigate *Energy*

Turn to Investigation file 5 p119

Aliens

1 Disappearance

MISSING!
Last week Clare Stanton disappeared from her home. Neighbours reported a strange light in the sky and police are investigating.

1 Match these words to a scene.
- get into the spaceship
- eat strange food
- pilot the spaceship
- wear a spacesuit
- visit their houses

2 🔲 **Listen to check.**

RETURNED
Clare Stanton turned up at her home yesterday. She claims that aliens from another galaxy kidnapped her. Tonight on Radio City, Clare talks about her incredible adventure.

3 Rewrite these sentences correctly.
1 They let me get into the spaceship.
2 They let me wear a spacesuit.
3 They made me visit their houses.
4 They let me eat strange food.
5 They made me pilot the spaceship.

>> 37 p122

2 Language study
make and *let*

1 Unjumble the sentences.

1 teacher . makes my do me homework
  a lot of
2 let parents my me . out week the during go

**2 What is the difference between *make*
and *let*?**

**3 Copy and complete the table with
information about yourself.**

	teacher	parent
make		
let		

4 Ask your partner about his/her table.
Example:
What do your parents make you do?
What do your parents let you do?

**5 Write two sentences about you and
your partner.**
Example:
1 *My parents make me tidy my room. Jo's
parents do not make him tidy his room, but they
make him go to bed early.*
2 *My parents let me go out during the week.
Jo's parents do not let him go out during the
week.*

3 Survey Teenage rights

**1 Answer the questions for yourself and then
interview two other students.**

Do your parents let you:
- wear what you want?
- watch what you want on television?
- go to bed late?
- have parties at home?
- eat what you want?

Do your parents make you:
- help at home?
- visit relatives at the weekend?
- do your homework before going to bed?
- go to bed early?
- have a shower every day?

2 Write a report with the information.
Example:
*David and Hilary's parents let them wear what they
want, but Jean's do not.*

4 What would you do?

1 Work in pairs to answer these questions.
1 If you were a teacher what would you make
  your students do?
2 If you were a teacher what would you let
  your students do?
Example:
*If I were a teacher I would make my students
wear a uniform.*

**2 Ask questions to find out what other pairs
wrote.**
Example:
What would you do if you were a teacher?
Would you make students do homework?

3 Which pair would be:
1 the strangest teacher?
2 the worst teacher?
3 the best teacher?

5 Story telling

**1 Work in pairs. Look at the picture and use
the phrases to write a short story about an
alien kidnapping.**
Well, yesterday at …
Then …
Next …
After that …
Finally …

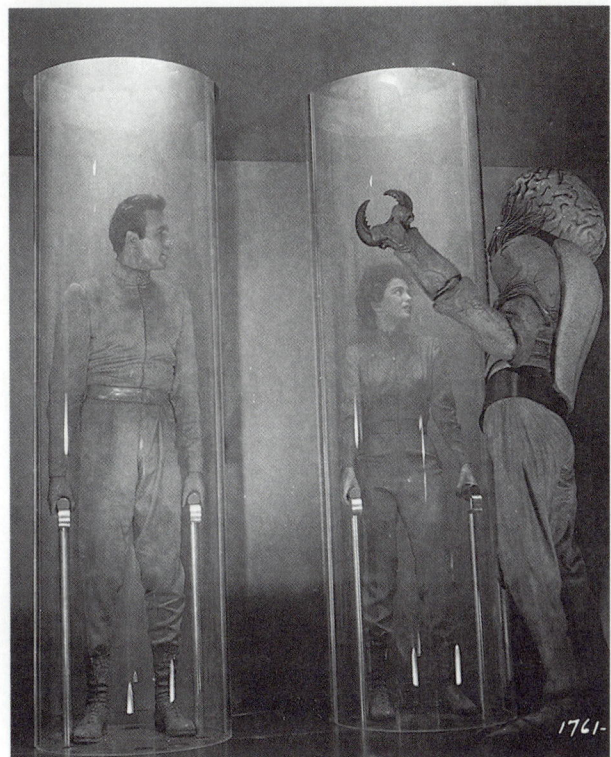

2 Tell your story to another pair.

6 Tune in 2B B2

1 🔲 **Listen. Copy and complete the note.**

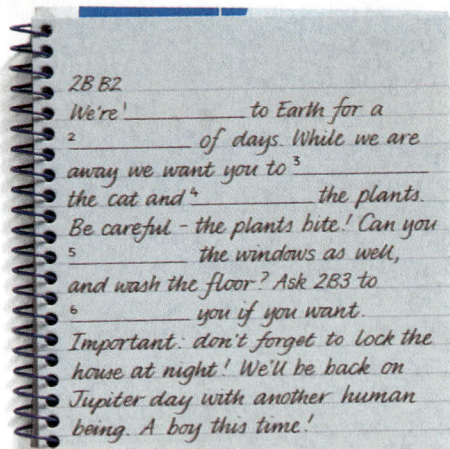

> 2B B2
> We're ¹_____ to Earth for a
> ²_____ of days. While we are
> away we want you to ³_____
> the cat and ⁴_____ the plants.
> Be careful - the plants bite! Can you
> ⁵_____ the windows as well,
> and wash the floor? Ask 2B3 to
> ⁶_____ you if you want.
> Important: don't forget to lock the
> house at night! We'll be back on
> Jupiter day with another human
> being. A boy this time!

2 What are the differences between the note and the instructions 2B B2 gives to 2B3?

»38 p122

7 Language study

want + object + infinitive

1 Copy the table and complete it with these words.

to clean I me you to
wash we him he her

subject pronoun	verb	object pronoun	infinitive
	want(s)		

2 Work in pairs. Write down something you want your partner to do.
Example:
I want him/her to open the window.

3 Mime the sentence to your partner.

4 Guess what your partner wants you to do.
Example:
Do you want me to open the window?

8 Game Alien sentences

1 Work in pairs. Rewrite this sentence and change two words.

I want you to speak Martian.

2 Give the new sentence to another pair.

3 Rewrite the sentence you receive, changing two more words. Continue until your teacher stops you.

4 Read the last sentence aloud. Who has the funniest sentence?

9 Sounds right

1 Listen to these sounds and words.

short	long
1 /ɪ/ sit	/ɪː/ see
2 /æ/ had	/aː/ hard
3 /ɒ/ not	/ɔː/ more
4 /ʊ/ full	/uː/ food

2 Copy the table and complete it with these words.

me you car tree choose bar put
cat want new ship dog saw fit

1	2	3	4	5	6	7	8
/ɪ/	/æ/	/ɒ/	/ʊ/	/ɪː/	/aː/	/ɔː/	/uː/

3 🔲 **Listen to check.**

4 Work in pairs.
A Draw the symbol of one of the sounds on your partner's back.
B Say the sound your partner draws.

10 Spot check

1 Find example sentences of these structures in the unit.
1 verb + object + infinitive without *to*
2 verb + object + infinitive

2 How are questions and negatives formed with these structures?

ASSIGNMENT 11
Humour

1 READING
Laughter

1 What is special about April 1st in England?

2 Read the text to check.

3 Work in pairs.

1 Do you have an April Fools' Day in your country? When is it?

2 Has anyone ever played an April Fools' joke on you? What was it? Did it make you laugh?

My girlfriend phoned me last week and invited me to a party at her house. She told me that it was a fancy-dress party and she wanted me to go as an escaped convict. I arranged to meet her there. When I arrived the house was very quiet. I waited for ten minutes, but people were looking at me in the street so I decided to go in. I rang the bell and to my surprise a real policeman opened the door. It was her uncle, a sergeant! He looked at me and laughed. He knew that it was April 1st, April Fools' Day! I was angry at first, but then I suddenly remembered that it was April Fools' Day and I laughed too.

2 LISTENING
Telling a joke

1 Unjumble the pictures to tell a joke.

2 📼 Listen to check. What is the punchline?

3 VOCABULARY *Sounds the same*

Homophones are words which sound the same as other words, but have a different spelling or meaning or both.

1 Find a homophone in the text for these words.
1 weak 2 meat 3 their 4 eye 5 four 6 new 7 two

2 Write a homophone for these words.
1 sea 2 ate 3 right 4 our

3 Explain the humour in this cartoon.

Why isn't the light on?

Because we're so bright!

4 FOLLOW UP

1 Work in groups. Write a joke you know in English.

2 Tell another group your joke.

3 Which was the funniest joke?

Holidays

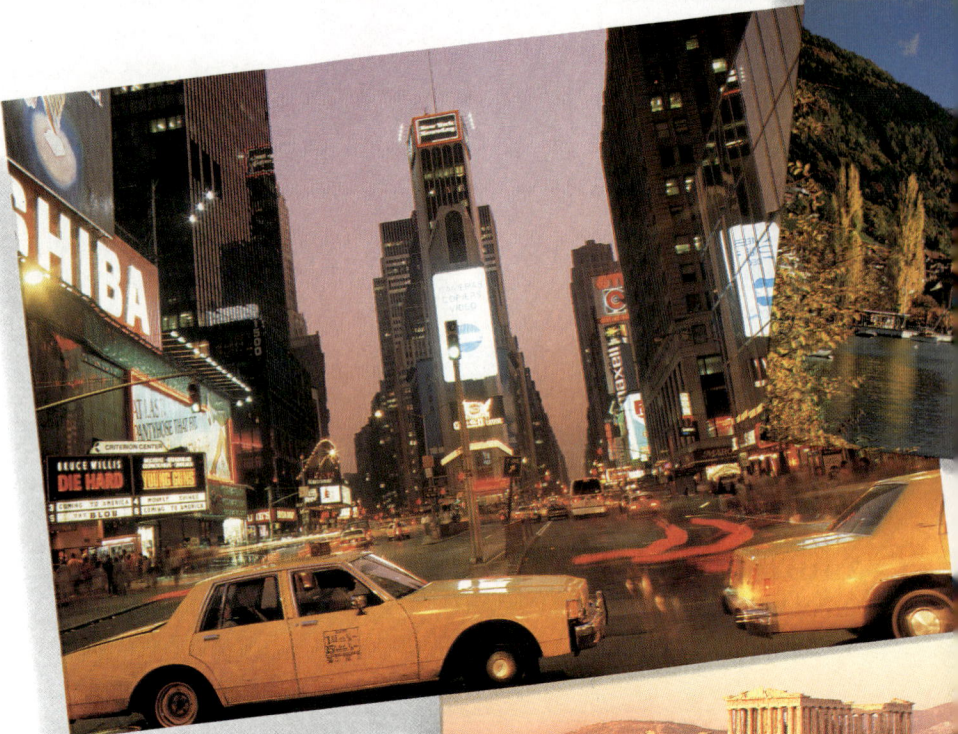

1 Places

1 Match the words to the appropriate postcards.

peaceful   lively   historic
noisy   touristy   unspoilt

2 Read the postcard. Which of the three places does it describe?

I'm having a fantastic holiday. Although it's a historic city, it's still a really lively place. I never get to bed before two! Debbie thinks it's too noisy, but she always complains about something! The people are very friendly and yesterday we met an interesting couple in a cafe, who showed us around the old part of town. I hope you aren't working too hard! I'll give you a ring when I get back.

Brenda
xx

Helen Jones
23 Old Coach Road
Breck Bridge
Chester
Great Britain

2 Language study Descriptions

1 How did Brenda and Debbie's friends ask them about:
1 the place   3 the people
2 the food   4 the weather
Example:
(1) the place   *What was the place like?*

2 Study the questions and answers.
A: What is your mother like?
B: She is very kind and understanding.
A: What does she like?
B: She likes modern music and fashion.

3 What is the difference between the two questions? What information is each one asking for?

3 What's it like?

1 Work in pairs. Copy the table and complete it with these words.
hot helpful warm intelligent clean
freezing crowded modern old-fashioned
cold kind good-looking ugly

people	place	weather

2 Complete these sentences.
1 The people in my class are ...
2 My town is ...
3 The weather at the moment is ...

3 Compare what you wrote with another pair.

4 In pairs, ask and answer questions about three other places in your country.
Example:
What is X like?

3 Answer these questions.
1 Where is Brenda?
2 What is the relationship between Brenda and Helen?
3 Who is Debbie?

4 📟 Listen to check.

5 Listen again. What are the differences between what Debbie says and what Brenda says?

6 Copy and complete the table with these words.
friendly   aggressive   fantastic   awful
boiling hot   sunny

	people	place	weather
Brenda			
Debbie			

4 Find out Last year

1 Work in pairs. Write questions to ask about your partner's last holiday
1 the accommodation   3 the weather
2 the food   4 the people
Example:
Where did you stay? - On a camp site.
What was it like? - It was very nice.

2 In pairs, ask and answer the questions.

>>> 39 p122

5 Tune in Booking a holiday

1 📷 **Listen. Which holiday are the customers interested in?**

1 a cruise in the fjords of Norway
2 a safari in Kenya
3 ten days in Indonesia

2 Listen again. Copy and complete the table.

	Sumatra	Java	Bali
number of days there	2		
how you get there		by coach	
cost per person			
dates		July - 21st July	

»40 p122

6 Language study

Polite requests

1 **What is different about these two requests?**
1 I want an ice-cream.
2 I'd like an ice-cream, please.

2 **Match the requests to the places.**
1 I'd like a double room, please.
2 I'd like a return to Manchester, please.
3 I'd like some information about holidays in India, please.
a travel agent
b hotel
c train station

3 **Unjumble the replies and match them to the requests above.**
1 you where ? certainly , like would to go
2 room like a view you with ? a would
3 smoking would ? like you non-smoking or

4 **In pairs practise the exchanges.**

7 Pairwork Travel agent

A Turn to PAIRWORK A30 p108
B Turn to PAIRWORK B27 p114

8 Situations On holiday

1 Match the words to a picture.
check in   box office   garage   beach

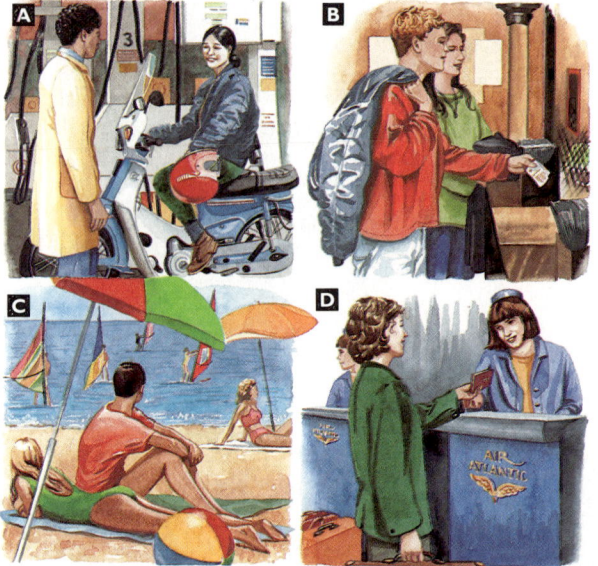

2 📷 **Listen. Where does the conversation take place?**

3 Work in pairs. How much of the dialogue can you remember?

4 Listen again to check.

5 Write a dialogue for one of the other situations. Act it out for another pair.

9 Dictation

A Turn to PAIRWORK A31 p108
B Turn to PAIRWORK B28 p114

10 Spot check

1 Use *like* to write questions for these answers.
1 It was wonderful, really hot and sunny.
2 Sunbathing.
3 I'd quite like to go to Thailand.
4 They were very friendly.

2 Look at your questions. Where is *like* a verb and where is it a preposition?

3 Find one more example of each type of question in the unit.

WRITING *Postcards*

1 Match the postcards to the holiday photographs.

I'm having a really relaxing holiday. The weather is fantastic and I've met a lot of really friendly people. The scenery is unspoilt and the food is delicious. Yesterday, I spent the day walking in the mountains and tomorrow I'm going on a boat trip. See you next week.
Love,
Anna xx

Clare Renton
14 Moor Drive
Lancaster
England

A

B

Hi!
I'm sitting on my balcony looking out over the
1 _____ streets. It's a
2 _____ place and the
people are very 3 _____.
The food is 4 _____!
Yesterday I went to a
5 _____ disco and I
didn't get back to the
hotel until three in the
morning. I'll probably go
there again tonight. I'm
having a 6 _____ time.
I'll tell you all about it
when I get back.
Alex

David Hunt
36 Park Road
Liverpool
GB

2 Work in pairs. Answer the questions.

1 What type of information is included in each of the postcards?
Example:
What Anna and Alex are doing at the moment.
2 Can we use contractions when we write a postcard?

3 Complete Alex's postcard with interesting adjectives. Compare what you wrote with your partner.

4 You are having your ideal holiday. Write a postcard to your partner about it.

Farewells

1 WESTGATE KIDS
EPISODE 8

1 What! I can't believe my eyes!

2 Shall I tell him or will you Mike?

You tell him. I have to go.

3 What's up?

4 I've just been offered a job in Birmingham.

Are you going to take it?

5 Why ask me?

6 It's a better job and more money.

7 When do we have to go?

At the end of next month.

8 That soon!

What about Susan?

Susan, I need to talk to you ...

9 But my dad hasn't been well. He needs a change.

10

1 Match the sentences to the appropriate scenes.

- I don't know. It'll affect everyone.
- You look miserable.
- I'll see you later.
- We'll have to move, you see.
- I want your opinion. I don't want to make the same mistake as last time.
- I wanted to talk to you about something important.
- What are you two doing?
- Look, I know your job here is difficult, but is the new job really worth it?
- Thanks for asking me for my opinion dad, but I need time to think.

2 🔲 **Listen to check.**

3 Answer these questions.
1 Why is Dave surprised to see Mike and Susan together?
2 Why does Mike have to leave?
3 What do Mike and his dad talk about?
4 Why does Mike feel sad?
5 What do you think Mike will say to Susan?

≫ 41 p122

2 Language study

Talking about the present

1 Find an example of these tenses in the *Westgate kids*.
1 simple present
2 present continuous
3 present perfect simple

2 Which tense do we use to talk about:
1 habits
2 actions happening now
3 routines
4 general past experience
5 recent news

3 Copy and complete the sentences with the correct form of the verbs in brackets.
1 I (like) listening to music.
2 I (study) English at the moment.
3 I (get up) at eight o'clock every morning.
4 I (be) to England twice in my life.
5 I (break) my leg.

4 Write questions for the sentences above. Interview your partner.
Example:
What do you like doing?

3 Student profiles

1 Write the names of two students.

2 Write sentences about:
1 the type of music they like
2 their favourite colour
3 the time they usually get up at the weekend
4 how often they go to discos
5 how many times they have been abroad
6 something interesting they have just done
7 what they are thinking about at the moment

3 Interview the students you wrote about.
Example:
What type of music do you like?

4 How many of the sentences you wrote were correct?

4 Role play

1 Work in groups. Choose one of these situations.
1 You are waiting for a bus.
2 You are travelling in an aeroplane.
3 You are lost in a jungle.

2 Use two or three of these expressions to write a short dialogue.
If I were you, I would ...
You shouldn't ...
Why don't you ...
What a pity!
I'm sorry, but I can't. I'm ...
Listen, I want you to ...
I don't agree. I think we should ...

5 Tune in I'll write

1 **Listen.**

2 What are Susan and Mike talking about?
- Mike's dad and his new job
- Susan's visit to Mike
- Susan's accident
- Matt
- Dave
- Susan's mum

42 p122

6 Language study Talking about the past and the future

1 What did Susan and Mike say? Copy and complete the sentences with the correct form of the verbs in brackets.
1 I (write).
2 I (come) to see you next week.
3 I (not see) Matt any more.
4 I (lie) in the road.
5 You (call) the ambulance.

2 **Listen again to check.**

3 Match the sentences to these descriptions.
a an action happening around a particular point in the past
b a planned action or intention
c a fixed future arrangement
d a confident prediction
e a completed past action

4 Write appropriate questions for the sentences.
Example:
Will Mike write to Susan?

5 In pairs, ask and answer the questions.

7 Dave's story

1 Unjumble the pictures to find the story.

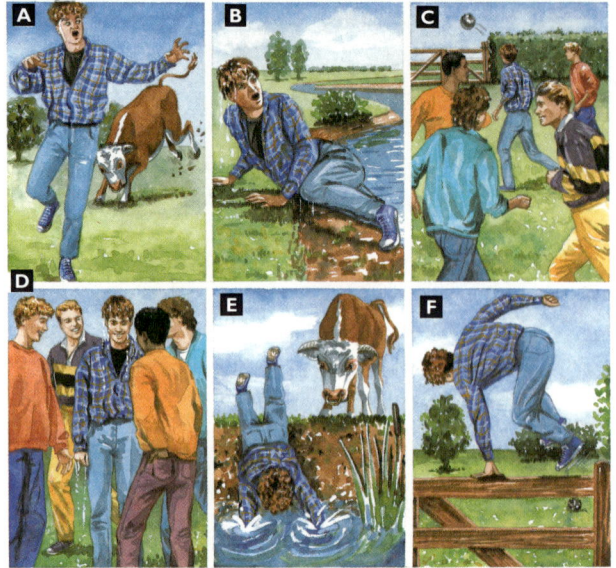

2 Write a paragraph about the school trip. Start like this:
We arrived at the camp site at ten o'clock.

8 Sounds right

1 Match the words to the appropriate vowel sounds.
eye leaving late sad smile bad while eight train cried
1/aɪ/ 2/iː/ 3/eɪ/ 4/æ/

2 **Listen. Write the words in the order you hear them.**

9 Spot check

1 Work in pairs. Write five questions to ask another pair about the events in the *Westgate kids* story.
Example:
What was Mike doing at the hospital in Unit 17?

2 You score ten points if you can answer the question without looking in your book. You score five points if you have to look and nothing if you are incorrect.

ASSIGNMENT 12
Travel

1 READING *Tickets*

1 Work in pairs. Match the descriptions to the appropriate pictures.
a bus ticket
b train ticket
c aeroplane ticket

2 Write six questions about the tickets. Give them to another pair to answer.
Example:
How much does the bus ticket cost?

2 LISTENING *Large numbers*

🔊 **Listen. Copy and complete the table.**

flight number	
speed	
height	
number of passengers	
flight time	
arrival time	

3 VOCABULARY *Multi-word fields*

1 Work in pairs. Copy and complete the vocabulary fields with these words.

wings   sail   handlebars   basket   hull   bonnet

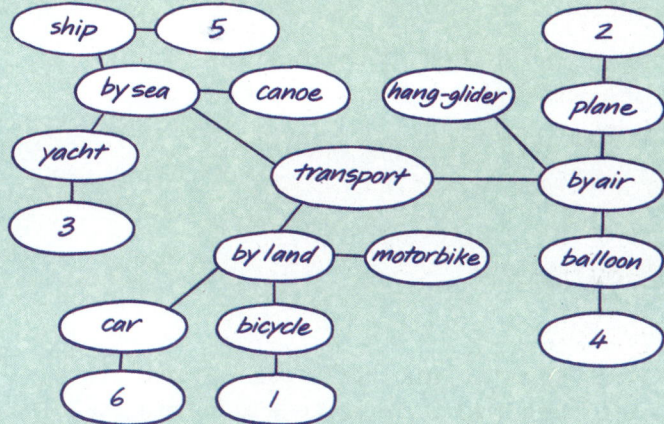

ship — 5
by sea — canoe
yacht
3
hang-glider
transport
2
plane
by air
by land — motorbike
balloon
car
bicycle
6
1
4

2 Add three more words.

3 Tell other pairs your words.

4 Choose a topic for a multi-word field.

5 Give it to another student to complete.

4 FOLLOW UP

1 Find out how people prefer travelling in your class.

1 on foot   5 by skateboard
2 by car   6 by aeroplane
3 by bike   7 by train
4 by bus   8 by boat

2 Make a poster with the information. Include a bar chart and pictures. Label the pictures.

Review and Extension 6

1 Grammar

■ Review of tenses

1 Copy the table.

Experience

Time		good	bad
	past		
	present		
	future		

2 Think of six experiences, one good and one bad, in the past, in the present and in the future.

3 Complete the table with a time expression for each experience.
Example: *two days ago, this week, tomorrow*

4 Look at your partner's table. Ask him/her questions about it.
Example:
What happened two days ago?

2 Vocabulary

Play the game in two groups, X and O.

1 On each square of the chart is the number of a unit. The object of the game is to place a X or a O on as many squares as possible.

1	4	7	10	13	16	19
2	5	8	11	14	17	20
3	6	9	12	15	18	21

2 Choose a word or a phrase from a unit shown on the chart.

3 Invent a question to ask the other group.
Example:
Unit 11 - *bicycle* - *How do you spell bicycle?*
Unit 11 - *rice* - *Name an uncountable food.*

3 In conversation

1 Work in pairs. Say these expressions in your language.

1. What's up?
2. What's your teacher like?
3. They make me go to bed at nine o'clock.
4. They let my brother come home very late.
5. You look miserable.

2 Think of a situation for a dialogue.
Example:
Two friends on a desert island.

3 Give it to another pair to write the dialogue.

4 Study skills Time for success

1 Work in pairs. Study this graph.

amount you remember

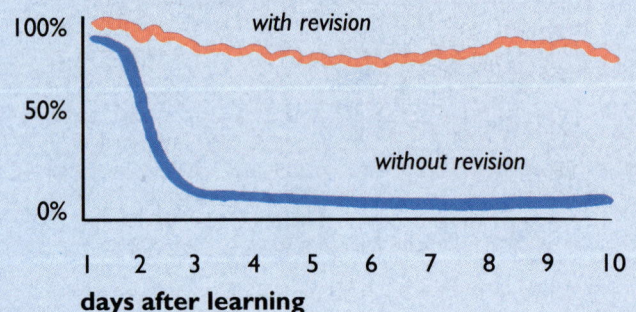

days after learning

The Ebbinghaus forgetting curve

2 Make your timetable for a typical week during your school holidays.

3 Write your social and leisure activities and your mealtimes.

4 Include time to revise and practise your English in your timetable. Remember: 'A little often is better than a lot infrequently.'

The Guardians
EPISODE 6

The Guardians!
Where are they?

Don't you understand?
We are the Guardians
now.

1 The adventure diary

Look at the pictures and use the prompts to complete the notes for Days 11 and 12.

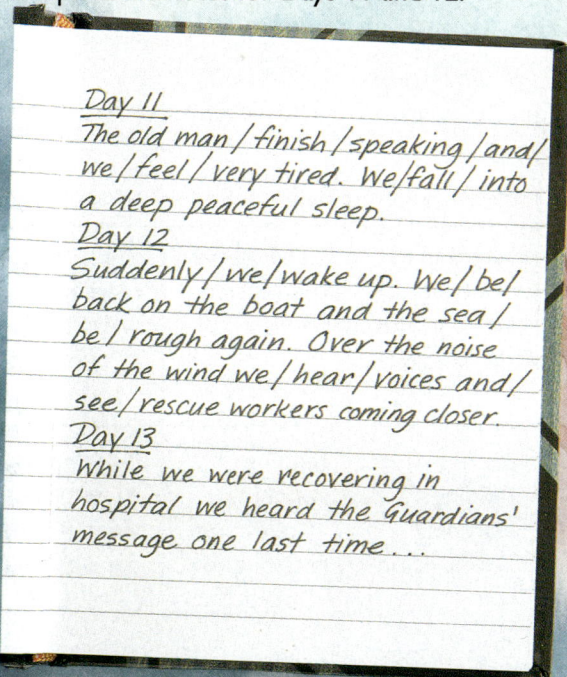

Day 11
The old man / finish / speaking / and / we / feel / very tired. We / fall / into a deep peaceful sleep.
Day 12
Suddenly / we / wake up. We / be / back on the boat and the sea / be / rough again. Over the noise of the wind we / hear / voices and / see / rescue workers coming closer.
Day 13
While we were recovering in hospital we heard the Guardians' message one last time...

2 Voices

Listen. What is the Guardians' message for young people?

3 Investigate *Recycling waste*

Turn to Investigation file 6 p120

A1

1   Work in groups of four.

2   One student chooses a famous person to be.

3   The other students ask Yes/No questions to find out who the person is.
Example:
Are you English? Yes, I am. / No, I'm not.

name	born	nationality	occupation
1 Helmut Kohl	1930	German	politician
2 Kylie Minogue	1968	Australian	singer
3 Michael Jordan	1962	American	basketball player
4 Sophia Loren	1934	Italian	actress
5 Naomi Campbell	1970	British	model

A2

1   You are at a party. Choose to be one of these people.

Ruth O'Leary
15
student
19 Brooke Road
Irish

Kevin Mills
20
football player
15 West Park
American

Karen Harris
19
musician
18 Trent Avenue
Scottish

Sara Gray
21
teacher
9 Queen Street
English

2   Use the information to have a conversation with your partner.

A3

Ask your partner questions about the people in his/her table (David, Marion, Judy, Clare, Stephen and Paul). Look at your table and find a suitable partner for each person.
Example:
Does David like reading?
(Yes, he does. / No, he doesn't.)

	Pam	John	Mary	Peter	Sally	Simon
Likes	reading watching television video games	reading watching television listening to music	watching television listening to music video games	listening to music video games the seaside	video games the seaside parties	the seaside reading watching television
Dislikes	listening to music the seaside parties	video games the seaside parties	the seaside parties reading	parties reading watching television	reading watching television listening to music	listening to music video games parties

A4

1 You are a pop star. Write an interesting name for yourself.

2 Copy and complete the card with information about yourself to answer your partner's questions.

```
✱ Name:
✱ Nationality:
✱ Address:
✱ Favourite type of music:
✱ Music I do not like:
✱ What I think about ...
   Madonna:
   Michael Jackson:
   Billy Idol:
✱ What I do at weekends:
```

3 Write questions to find the information above.
Example:
What is your name?
Where are you from?

4 Interview your partner with the questions.

A5

1 Describe the pictures to your partner.

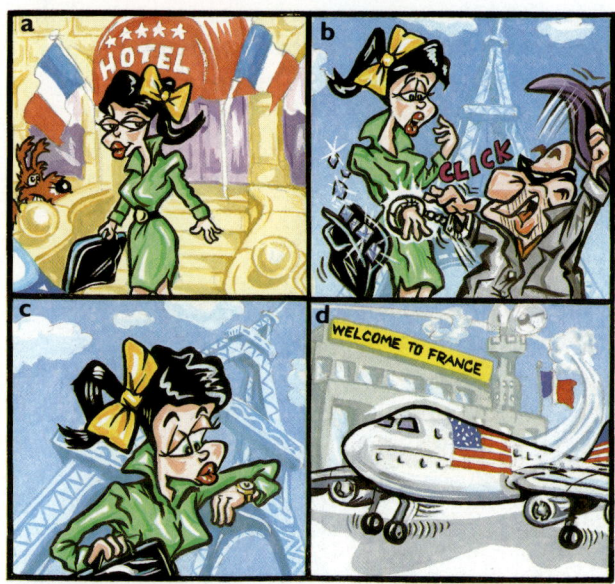

a leave/hotel
b Magnut/arrest/Lola
c wait/Eiffel Tower
d arrive/airport

2 Unjumble these and your partner's pictures to find the story.

3 Write the story.

A6

1 Dictate these sentences to your partner.
An old woman is sitting on a chair. She's reading a book. She's got short dark hair. She's wearing a white shirt and a blue skirt.

2 Write what your partner dictates to you.

3 Look at the picture. Correct your partner's sentences.
Example:
The man isn't old. He's young.
He isn't walking in the park. He's watching television.

A7

1 Unjumble the words in the questions.
1 old ? new or the was car
2 time competition did what the start ?
3 fans cheer ? her did
4 cry won when she ? she gold medal the did
5 javelin ? did find where she the

2 As your partner reads the story ask him/her appropriate questions.

3 Retell the story with the new information.

A8

1 In turns, dictate each line of the dialogue to your partner.
A: Did ____ see Aliens 3 ____ ____?
B: ____, I ____.
A: What ____ you ____ of ____ ?
B: I ____ it was ____.
A: I ____ think ____.
B: But ____ very ____.
A: ____, but ____ exciting!
B: I ____ agree.
A: ____ did you ____ it ____?
B: I ____.
A: But ____ said ...
B: I ___ the ___ part and then ___ ___ to bed.

2 Practise the dialogue in pairs.

103

A9

1 You are organising a party one day next week when John, Helen, Mary and Graham are free. Ask your partner questions about what John and Helen are doing next week.
Example:
What is John doing on Monday?

	Mary	Graham
Monday		cinema
Tuesday		
Wednesday	visit uncle	dentist
Thursday		babysitting
Friday	restaurant	
Saturday		
Sunday	visit Tony and Jill	

2 Answer your partner's questions about Mary and Graham.

A10

You have part of the electronic code to enter Dr Rufus' laboratory. Your partner has the other part. Dictate your sentences to your partner. Who can find the key first?

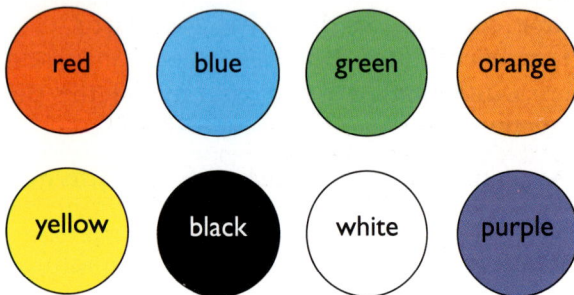

red	blue	green	orange
yellow	black	white	purple

1 You should press the white and black buttons after the green one.
2 You should press the orange button after the yellow one.
3 You should press the red button after the blue one.

A11

1 You are the editor of a newspaper. You are looking for a journalist to work for you. Copy the table and tick (✔) the type of experience you want the journalist to have.

	yes
played football professionally	
been a singer	
travelled around Europe	
done a computer course	
studied Arabic	
climbed a mountain	

2 Interview your partner. Ask him/her questions about the information in your table.
Example:
Have you ever played football professionally?
When?
Who for?

3 If your partner is not suitable for the job, interview another student (B) to find someone who is suitable.

A12

These three people all have a twin. The twins have had the same experiences recently. Ask your partner questions to find the name of the twin for each person below.
Example:
Has anyone just passed an exam?

Mary
Has just passed an exam.
Has just won some money.
Has just got married.
Has just found a new job.

Harold
Has just passed an exam.
Has just won some money.
Has just got married.
Has just bought a new house.

Susan
Has just passed an exam.
Has just won some money.
Has just found a new job.
Has just bought a new house.

A13

1 Dictate this part of the letter to your partner.

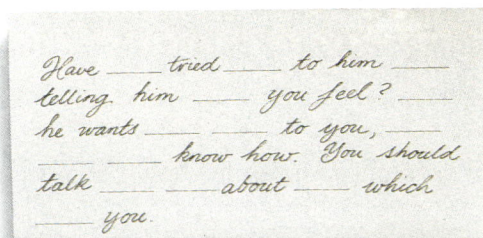

Have _____ tried _____ to him _____
telling him _____ you feel? _____
he wants _____ _____ to you, _____
_____ _____ know how. You should
talk _____ _____ about _____ which
_____ you.

2 Copy this part of the letter and complete it with the words your partner dictates to you.

3 What is the problem?

4 Does the letter contain good advice?

A14

1 Write a different job for each sentence.
1 You have to wear a uniform.
2 You do not have to wear a uniform.
3 You have to help people.
4 You have to sell things.
5 You have to travel a lot.
6 You do not have to travel a lot.

2 Read the jobs you wrote to your group. If you wrote a different job from the others in your group, you win five points.

3 Choose one of the jobs and write as many sentences about it as possible in five minutes.
Example:
You have to wear a uniform.
Policeman - You have to keep the peace.

4 Read your sentences to your group. Who has the most correct sentences?

A15

1 Read the information about marathon runners and complete the sentence with four food words.

Marathon runners need a lot of stamina. Serious marathon runners run five or six times a week. They do not train in gyms with weights very much. They eat a lot of carbohydrates as part of their normal diet. They eat foods such as _____, _____, _____ and _____. On race days they do not eat much, but during a race it is very important for them to drink a lot of water.

2 Answer your partner's questions.

3 Use the prompts to ask your partner about weight lifters.
1 What/need/to develop?
2 How long/spend/gym?
3 Train/outside/gym?
4 Eat/a lot of/carbohydrates?
5 Why/eat/protein?
Example:
What do weight lifters need to develop?

A16

1 You are a doctor. Write three questions to ask your patient about:
a food and diet
b exercise
c sleep
Example:
What do you eat for breakfast?

2 Write a piece of advice for each category.
Example:
You should eat a lot of fruit.

3 Ask your patient your questions and give him/her some advice.

A17

1 Dictate these sentences to your partner.
1 Paul gets too much sleep.
2 Veronica eats lots of fruit and vegetables.
3 Sonia goes to a lot of parties.
4 Steve spends most of his time in the gym.

2 Match each sentence your partner dictates to a diagram.
exercise = 🟩   healthy diet = 🟧
relaxation = 🟧   fun = 🟥

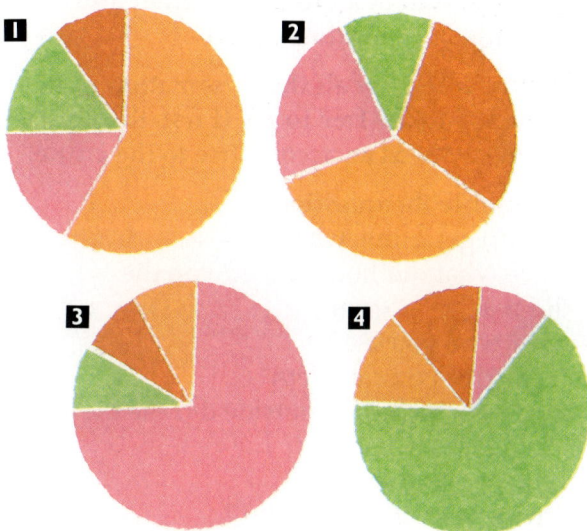

105

1 Write sentences about the picture with these words.

sleep play jump chase eat fight
Example: *The black cat is sleeping in the fish bowl.*

2 How many differences are there between your picture and your partner's? Ask questions.
Example:
Where is the black cat?
What is it doing?

A19

1 Copy and complete this statement with your own words.

I got up at _____ . I left the house at _____ and went to the bus stop. On my way I saw two _____ . One was _____ and the other was _____ . The _____ one had a gun. They stopped outside the bank for _____ and then went in. Then the _____ one came running out and a minute later the _____ one ran out and fired a shot into the air. It was _____ o'clock. The police arrived _____ later.

2 Give the statement to your partner and answer his/her questions.

3 If you remember all the information in your statement you are free to go! If not, the police will arrest you as an accomplice to the crime.

4 Unjumble the questions.
1 you up get ? time what did
2 leave what did house time ? you the
3 did where ? go you
4 did ? who you see
5 ? describe you can them
6 long how bank stop outside did the they ?
7 ? happened what next
8 ? time what it was
9 arrive when the police did ?

5 Look at your partner's statement and ask him/her your questions. If your partner's answers are the same as the statement he/she is free to go. If the answers are different, arrest him/her as an accomplice to the crime.

A20

The first sentence represents how you see yourself.
The second sentence represents your emotional life.
The third sentence represents how you see your life at the moment.
The fourth sentence represents how you see your future.
The fifth sentence represents what you will be like in the future.
The sixth sentence represents your future fortune.

A21

1 Dictate these sentences to your partner.
1 I have just finished a fantastic book.
2 At the top of the letter is an address.
3 The old woman is happy to see her.
4 The girl receives a mysterious letter.
5 The old woman tells her a story.

2 Unjumble these and your partner's sentences to find the story.

3 Use *that*, *which* or *who* to join your sentences your partner's.
Example: *I have just finished a fantastic book that my brother lent me.*

A22

Twenty questions
Play the game in groups. One player thinks of the name of an animal, mineral or vegetable. The other players have to find out what it is by asking Yes/No questions. They can ask only twenty questions.

A23

1 Choose a situation. Read it to the others in your group.
1 The headmaster's door is open and nobody is in the room.
2 My mum and dad go away for the weekend.
3 I find my best friend's secret diary.

2 Choose the piece of advice you think is most suitable. Change roles with the person who gave it.

A24

1 Dictate these sentences to your partner.

What's the matter?

If I were you, I'd write him/her a letter.

Are you OK?

What about cheering up now!

Oh, come on! Why don't you ring him/her up tonight?

2 Write the sentences your partner dictates to you. Unjumble the dialogue and practise it in pairs.

A25

1 🔲 **Listen. Copy and complete the sentences.**

Mum, 1____ I ask you something?

2____ I go out with Mike 3____?

Yes, he's 4____ me to go to the cinema.

5____ 9.30.

Is it OK 6____ we go to a coffee bar after?

Oh, Mum! We'll only go 7____ half an hour.

8 ____ Mum!

2 Practise the dialogue with your partner.

A26

You are your partner's son/daughter. Write five things you would like to do at the weekend. Ask your mother/father for permission to do these things. Write five questions.

Use *Can I ...?, Is it OK if I ...?, Could I ...?*

A27

1 Unjumble the second part of these sentences.

1 The RB 2000 ...   least is the expensive

2 The TS 50 ...   is as AX 4 expensive as not the

3 The RB 2000 ...   up-to-date the is more TS 50 than

4 The ZT-100 ...   RB 2000 powerful less than is the

5 The AX 4 ...   as as not use is RB 2000 the easy to

2 Read the sentences to your partner. Copy and complete the star rating table.

(★★★★ excellent, ★★★ good, ★★ fair, ★ poor)

	Good value?	Powerful?	Easy to use?	Up-to-date?
RB 2000				
TS 50				
AX4				
ZT-I00				

A28

1 Choose one of these people.

J.F. Kennedy

Marie Curie

Cervantes

2 Write a sentence about the person. Do not write the person's name.

Example:

He used to be a politician.

3 Read your sentence to your partner and answer his/her questions.

4 Ask your partner questions to find the person he/she chose.

Example:

Did she use to be an actress?

A29

1 Read this passage to your partner.

People had to be very rich to buy cars at the beginning of the century. In 1920, a basic car cost about £500, but in 1925 Henry Ford reduced the price of his famous Model T Ford to £185. By the 1930s it was possible to buy a car for about £100.

2 Listen to your partner. Find the mistakes in the passage below.

People used to travel by horse or stagecoach after the railways became the main form of transport in the United States. By 1987 the USA had 100,000 miles of roads. People did not use to travel all over the USA by rail until the car became popular. Nowadays most people travel long distances by car.

3 Rewrite the passage correctly.

1 You are a travel agent. Read the information in the leaflet.

2 Try to sell your partner the most expensive holiday. Answer his/her questions. Start like this:
Certainly. There are two special offers at the moment.

3 Change roles. You want to go on holiday. Your partner is a travel agent and you want to find out what type of holiday he/she has to offer.

4 Write questions to find out about:
a place   d activities
b type of holiday   e dates
c accommodation   f price

5 Start the conversation like this:
I'd like some information about summer holidays.

SPECIAL SUMMER OFFERS!

★ **Place: the Amazon**
Type of holiday: *adventure*
Accommodation: *tent*
Activities: *canoeing, walking in the jungle, climbing*
Dates: *first or second week in July*
Price: **£3,000**

★ **Place: Egypt**
Type of holiday: *sightseeing*
Accommodation: *1 and 2-star hotels*
Activities: *tours to the pyramids and other places of interest*
Dates: *ten days at the beginning of September*
Price: **£2,000**

A31

1 Ask your partner questions to complete your ticket.

Date	Depart	Arrive	Other	Baggage Allowance
21/08/93	Milan Linate ____	London Heathrow 0710	via ____	20kg
Return __/08/93	London Heathrow ____	Milan Linate 1100	via Geneva	20kg

2 You have won a free holiday in a quiz programme. Tell your partner where you have decided to go and why.

A32

1 You are a little angel! Listen to A and give him/her some angelic advice.

2 If he/she takes your advice, change roles.

PAIRWORK B

B1

1 You are at a party. Choose to be one of these people.

Garry Jones
20
shop assistant
3 Castle Street
Welsh

Gareth Cooper
18
student
13 Dock Road
Australian

Kate Brent
23
nurse
28 Green Lane
Canadian

Roger Fry
21
policeman
9 Kingsway
English

2 Use the information to have a conversation with your partner.

B2

Ask your partner questions about the people in his/her table (Pam, John, Mary, Peter, Sally, and Simon). Look at your table and find a suitable partner for each person.
Example:
Does Pam like reading? (Yes, she does. / No, she doesn't.)

	David	Marion	Judy	Clare	Stephen	Paul
Likes	listening to music video games the seaside	video games the seaside parties	reading watching television listening to music	watching television listening to music video games	the seaside reading watching television	reading watching television video games
Dislikes	parties reading watching television	reading watching television listening to music	video games the seaside parties	the seaside parties reading	listening to music video games parties	listening to music the seaside parties

B3

1 You are going to interview a pop star. Write questions to find the information for the card.
Example:
What is your name?
Where are you from?

2 Interview your partner.

3 You are a pop star. Write an interesting name for yourself.

4 Copy and complete the card with information about yourself to answer your partner's questions.

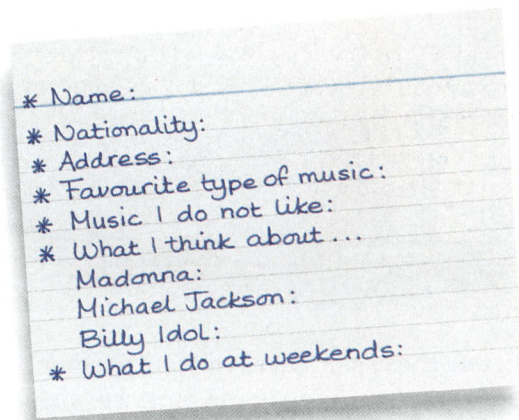

* Name:
* Nationality:
* Address:
* Favourite type of music:
* Music I do not like:
* What I think about ...
  Madonna:
  Michael Jackson:
  Billy Idol:
* What I do at weekends:

B4

1 Describe the pictures to your partner.

a get into/taxi
b give/diamonds/strange man
c policemen/take Lola away
d meet/strange man

2 Unjumble these and your partner's pictures to find the story.

3 Write the story.

B5

1 Write what your partner dictates to you.

2 Look at the picture. Correct your partner's sentences.
Example:
The woman isn't old. She's young. She isn't sitting on a chair. She's standing at a bus stop.

3 Dictate these sentences to your partner.
An old man is walking in the park. He's looking at the flowers. He's got short hair. He's wearing a brown jacket and trousers.

B6

Unjumble the pictures to find the story. Write a sentence for each picture. Tell the story to your partner. Start like this:
Last week Karen had an accident. She ...

1 win gold medal

2 fans cheer

3 competition start

4 arrive/stadium/car

5 throw javelin/javelin disappear

6 find javelin

B7

1 In turns, dictate each line of the dialogue to your partner.

A: ____ you ____ ____ last night?
B: Yes, ____ did.
A: ____ did ____ think ____ it?
B: ____ thought ____ ____ terrible.
A: ____ didn't ____ so.
B: ____ it was ____ violent.
A: Yes, ____ that's____!
B: ____ don't ____.
A: Why ____ ____ watch ____ then?
B: ____ didn't.
A: ____ you ____ ....
B: ____ saw ____ first ____ ____ ____ I went ____ ____.

2 Practise the dialogue in pairs.

B8

1 You are organising a party one day next week when John, Helen, Mary and Graham are free. Ask your partner questions about what Mary and Graham are doing next week.
Example:*What is Mary doing on Monday?*

	John	Helen
Monday	concert	theatre
Tuesday		tennis
Wednesday	football	
Thursday		
Friday		
Saturday		
Sunday	cycling	

2 Answer your partner's questions about John and Helen.

B9

You have part of the electronic code to enter Dr Rufus' laboratory. Your partner has the other part. Dictate your sentences to your partner. Who can find the key first?

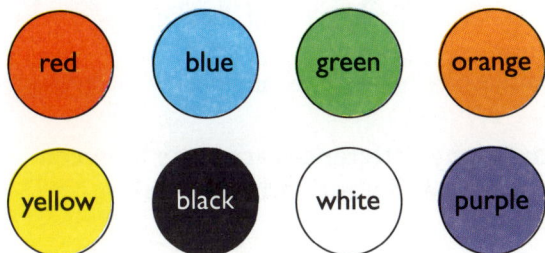

red   blue   green   orange
yellow   black   white   purple

1 You should not press the black button after the yellow one.
2 You should press the black and yellow buttons after the white one.
3 You should press the blue button after the orange one.
4 You should press the purple button last.

B10

1 You are a journalist looking for a job. Copy the table and tick (✔) the type of experience you have.

	yes
played football professionally	
been a singer	
travelled around Europe	
done a computer course	
studied Arabic	
climbed a mountain	

2 For each experience think about answers to questions beginning:
When? / Why? / Who? / Where?

3 Answer your partner's questions.

B11

These three people all have a twin. The twins have had the same experiences recently. Ask your partner questions to find the name of the twin for each person below.
Example:
Has anyone just passed an exam?

David
Has just passed an exam.
Has just won some money.
Has just got married.
Has just bought a new house.

Carol
Has just passed an exam.
Has just won some money.
Has just found a new job.
Has just bought a new house.

Francis
Has just passed an exam.
Has just won some money.
Has just got married.
Has just found a new job.

B12

1 Dictate this part of the letter to your partner.

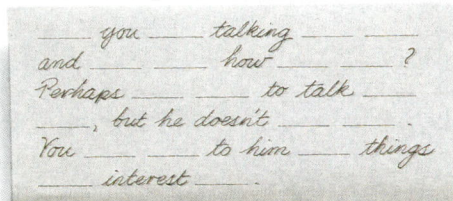

2 Copy this part of the letter and complete it with the words your partner dictates to you.

3 What is the problem? Does the letter contain good advice?

B13

1 Use the prompts to ask your partner about marathon runners.
1 What/need?
2 How often/run?
3 What/normally eat?
4 What/eat/on race days?
5 How much water/drink/during a race?
Example: *What do marathon runners need?*

111

2 Read the information about weight lifters and complete the sentence with four food words.

> Weight lifters need to develop very strong muscles. Professional weight lifters spend eight to ten hours a day in the gym. They do not train outside the gym very much. It is also very important that they eat the right kind of food. Stamina is not as important for weight lifters as marathon runners, so they do not need to eat a lot of carbohydrates. They do need to eat a lot of protein because it helps build up their muscles. Generally they eat a lot of ____, ____, ____ and ____.

B14

1 You are very unhealthy! Read the text about your life.

> I have a very large breakfast. I usually eat eight pieces of toast with chocolate spread and drink five cups of coffee with three sugars in each. After breakfast I watch television and then I take a taxi to the newsagent and buy two bars of chocolate. When I get home I eat lunch. Generally I eat a lot of meat and I never eat fruit or vegetables. For dessert I have a large piece of cake or pie. Then my friend comes round and we play cards all afternoon. I watch television in the evening and eat a lot of biscuits and crisps. I go to bed at ten o'clock. I feel so tired today, I have decided to go to the doctor.

2 Visit the doctor and answer his/her questions.

B15

1 Match each sentence your partner dictates to a diagram.

exercise = ■   healthy diet = ■
relaxation = ■   fun = ■

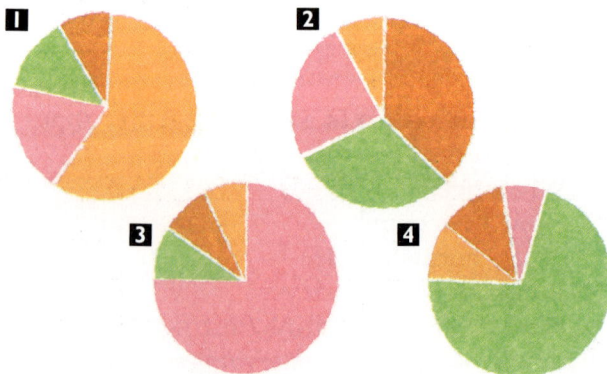

2 Dictate these sentences to your partner.
a Frank eats too many sweets.
b Jenny does not do enough exercise.
c Bill spends too much time asleep.
d Donna watches too much television.

B16

1 Write sentences about the picture with these words.
eat play chase crawl fight
Example:
The black cat is eating a fish next to the fish bowl.

2 How many differences are there between your picture and your partner's? Ask questions.
Example:
Where is the black cat?
What is it doing?

B17

1 Unjumble the questions.
1 you up get ? time what did
2 leave what did house time ? you the
3 did where ? go you
4 did ? who you see
5 ? describe you can them
6 long how bank stop outside did the they ?
7 ? happened what next
8 ? time what it was
9 arrive when the police did ?

2 Look at your partner's statement and ask him/her your questions. If your partner's answers are the same as the statement he/she is free to go. If the answers are different, arrest him/her as an accomplice to the crime.

3 Copy and complete this statement with your own words.

I got up at _____ . I left the house at _____ and went to the bus stop. On my way I saw two _____ . One was _____ and the other was _____ . The _____ one had a gun. They stopped outside the bank for _____ and then went in. Then the _____ one came running out and a minute later the _____ one ran out and fired a shot into the air. It was _____ o'clock. The police arrived _____ later.

4 Give the statement to your partner and answer his/her questions.

5 If you remember all the information in your statement you are free to go! If not, the police will arrest you as an accomplice to the crime.

B18

1 Dictate these sentences to your partner.
1 The book is about a girl.
2 She goes there and meets an old woman.
3 My brother lent me the book.
4 The story changes her life.
5 The address is in an old part of her town.

2 Unjumble these and your partner's sentences to find the story.

3 Use that, which or who to join your sentences your partner's.
Example: *I have just finished a fantastic book that my brother lent me.*

B19

One minute!
Play the game in groups. Write down the name of a television programme. You have one minute to make as many different words with the letters in the name as possible. You can use the letters more than once.

B20

1 You are a little devil! Listen to A and give him/her some devilish advice.

2 If he/she takes your advice, change roles.

B21

1 Dictate these sentences to your partner.
No, I'm not.
I can't. I'm too nervous.
That's a good idea!
OK, I'll try.
It's Andy/Andrea. He/she doesn't like me.

2 Write the sentences your partner dictates to you. Unjumble the dialogue and practise it in pairs.

B22

1 Listen. Copy and complete the sentences.
What 1____ it?
Mike? The boy 2____ the hospital?
What time 3____ it 4____ ?
All right 5____ .
A coffee bar! No, Susan you 6____ ! Remember your accident. You 7____ go to the cinema but you 8____ to come home straight after that.
Well, OK. 9____ be careful.

2 Practise the dialogue with your partner.

B23

Your partner will ask your permission to do five things. Refuse to give your permission. Use five different reasons.

B24

1 Unjumble the second part of these sentences.
1 The ZT-100 ... the most is expensive
2 The AX 4 ... up-to-date as as not is TS 50 the
3 The ZT-100 ... is to use easier the than TS 50
4 The AX 4 ... powerful is than more ZT-100 the
5 The TS 50 ... powerful least the is

2 Read the sentences to your partner. Copy and complete the star rating table.
(★★★★ excellent, ★★★ good, ★★ fair, ★ poor)

	Good value?	Powerful?	Easy to use?	Up-to-date?
RB 2000				
TS 50				
AX4				
ZT-100				

B25

1 Ask your partner questions to find the person he/she chose.
Example:
Did he use to write poetry?

2 Choose one of these people.
El Cid
Marilyn Monroe
Elvis Presley

3 Write a sentence about the person. Do not write the person's name.
Example:
He used to ride a white horse.

4 Read your sentence to your partner and answer his/her questions.

B26

1 Listen to your partner. Find the mistakes in the passage below.

> People did not have to be very rich to buy cars at the beginning of the century. In 1920, a basic car cost about £1,000 and in 1945 Henry Ford increased the price of his famous Model E Ford to £1,500. By the 1930s it was not possible to buy a car for less than £2000.

2 Read this passage to your partner.

> People used to travel by horse or stagecoach before the railways became the main form of transport in the United States. By 1897 the USA had 100,000 miles of railway track. People used to travel all over the USA by rail until the car became popular. Nowadays most people travel long distances by air.

3 Rewrite the first passage correctly.

B27

1 You want to go on a cheap holiday. Your partner is a travel agent and you want to find out what type of holiday he/she has to offer.

2 Write questions to find out about:
a place   d activities
b type of holiday e dates
c accommodation   f price

3 Start the conversation like this:
I'd like some information about summer holidays.

4 Change roles. You are a travel agent. Read the information in the leaflet.

SPECIAL SUMMER OFFERS!

★ Place: **Switzerland**
Type of holiday: *skiing*
Accommodation: *self-catering*
Activities: *skiing*
Dates: *last two weeks of July*
Price: **£2,500**

★ Place: **the Caribbean**
Type of holiday: *beach*
Accommodation: *on a yacht*
Activities: *water sports and sightseeing*
Dates: *ten days at the end of August*
Price: **£3,800**

5 Try to sell your partner the most expensive holiday. Start like this:
Certainly. There are two special offers at the moment

B28

1 Ask your partner questions to complete your ticket.

Date	Depart	Arrive	Other	Baggage Allowance
__/08/93	Milan Linate 0640	London Heathrow	via Paris	20kg
Return 28/08/93	London Heathrow 0830	Milan Linate	via ____	20kg

2 You have won a free holiday in a quiz programme. Tell your partner where you have decided to go and why.

The Guardians
INVESTIGATION FILE 1

1 WORD SEARCH

Match each word to its sound and translation.

a greenhouse (n) f /ˈaɪsˌkæp/ k inundaciones
b icecap (n) g /flʌd/ l fundir
c melt (v) h /ˈsiːˌlev(ə)l/ m invernadero
d sea level (n) i /ˈgriːnˌhaʊs/ n niveles del mar
e flood (n) j /melt/ o casquetes de hielo

2 THE WEATHER

1 Match the words to a picture.
rain sunshine snow wind clouds

2 Listen. Match the weather forecasts to the seasons.
summer autumn winter spring

3 Copy and complete these sentences from the winter forecast.
1 It _____ be cold and wet this evening in the North.
2 Tomorrow _____ continue cloudy.
3 Temperatures _____ rise above 6°C.

4 Write tomorrow's weather forecast for your country.

3 THE GREENHOUSE EFFECT

1 Label the diagram with these words.
sun's rays Earth layer of gases pollution

2 Read these questions.

1 How much will the Earth's temperature rise by 2030?
2 What will happen to vast areas of land?
3 What will happen to the icecaps?
4 What will happen as a result?

3 Read the text to find the answers.

Pollution is gradually changing the balance of gases in the Earth's atmosphere. Scientists predict that the Earth's temperature will rise between 1.5°C and 3°C by the year 2030. This will change the world's climate.

The effects on agriculture will be profound and vast areas of land will become desert. Also, icecaps will melt and as a result sea levels will rise by more than 1.5 metres creating serious floods in many countries.

4 ACTION FILE

Avoid buying aerosols with CFC gases in them.

1 Match the slogans to a piece of information.
1 Conserve fossil fuels.
2 Protect rainforests.
3 Use natural energy.
4 Ban CFC gases.

a Aerosols which contain CFC gases increase the greenhouse effect and destroy the outer layer of the Earth's atmosphere - the ozone.

b Solar power, wind power and hydro-electric power provide effective and non-polluting sources of energy.

c Trees help to convert carbon dioxide into oxygen. We need to plant more trees to stop the build up of carbon dioxide in the atmosphere which damages the ozone layer and causes the greenhouse effect.

d Burning coal gas and oil increases the level of carbon dioxide in the atmosphere. We need to control the amounts of these fuels that we use.

2 Use the information to make a poster.

CLIMATE

SEAS

HABITAT

ENERGY

RICH & POOR

WASTE

The Guardians
INVESTIGATION FILE 2

SEAS

HABITAT

ENERGY

RICH & POOR

WASTE

1 WORD SEARCH

Match each word to its sound and translation.

a brain (n)	h /ˈpaʊəfʊl/	o respirar
b surface (n)	i /ˈʃæləʊ/	p poco profundo
c breathe (v)	j /breɪn/	q superficie
d shallow (adj)	k /ɜːn/	r red
e powerful (adj)	l /ˈsɜːfɪs/	s ganar
f earn (v)	m /net/	t cerebro
g net (n)	n /briːð/	u potente

2 LIFE AT SEA

1 Are these statements true or false?

1 Dolphins live solitary lives.
2 A dolphin's brain is bigger than a human's.
3 A dolphin can swim faster than 30 kilometres per hour.
4 Whales have warm blood.
5 A blue whale is the largest living mammal.
6 Whales do not sing.

Read the passage to check.

There are over 30 different species of dolphin. They live in groups and communicate with each other in a complex language. They are very intelligent creatures and a dolphin's brain is bigger than a human's. An average dolphin is more than 2 metres long and can swim faster than 45 kilometres per hour.

Whales are mammals, not fish, so they are warm-blooded and have to come to the surface to breathe. The blue whale is the largest living mammal. It is over 30 metres long and weighs 160 tonnes. Whales are very intelligent creatures and communicate with each other by singing.

3 DOLPHINS IN DANGER

Read the passage and write five questions about it to ask another pair.
Example:
When did fishermen fish near the shore?

Forty years ago fishermen fished near the shore in small boats. Then there were a lot of fish in the shallow waters, but nowadays stocks are low and fishermen go further out to sea to find them. In order to do this they buy bigger and more powerful boats. These boats are very expensive and fishermen need to catch much larger quantities of fish to earn enough money to pay for their boats and equipment. The larger the boats fishermen use, the larger their nets will be. This means that the nets catch all kinds of different sea creatures, not just fish. Thousands of dolphins die every year in this way.

4 ACTION FILE

Visit your local zoo and find out about the animals that live there.

Choose one of the projects below.

A
1 Find some pictures and articles about whales, dolphins or pollution at sea.
2 Write a summary of one article in English.
3 Display your work as a poster.

B
1 Design a 'Save the whale' or 'Save the dolphin' badge.

116

The Guardians
INVESTIGATION FILE 3

HABITAT

ENERGY

RICH & POOR

WASTE

1 WORD SEARCH

Match each word to its sound and translation.

a avoid (v)	e /fiːd/	i extinto
b feed (v)	f /lʌŋ/	j alimentar
c extinct (adj)	g /əˈvɔɪd/	k evitar
d lung (n)	h /ɪkˈstɪŋkt/	l pulmón

2 NATURAL HABITATS

1 Match the animals to a habitat.

savannah	tundra	woods of Europe
rainforest	desert	

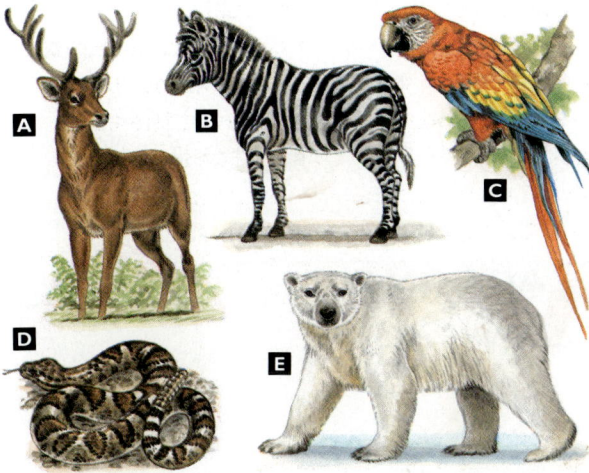

2 Match each habitat with its appropriate description.

A Snakes and other reptiles are very common. Small mammals usually live in holes to avoid the heat.

B Red deer and wild boar live among the trees.

C Antelope, zebra and buffalo feed on the grasses, while elephants and giraffes feed on the trees. Predators include lions and hyenas.

D Monkeys, parrots and snakes live here as well as a rich variety of insects, including many species which are still unidentified.

E Polar bears and arctic foxes are two of the resident animals. They are capable of surviving long, cold winters when there is not much food.

3 RAINFORESTS IN DANGER

1 Are these statements true or false?
1. Rainforests are found on all the continents.
2. Half of the world's species of insects live in the rainforests.
3. In the last 40 years, 80 per cent of the world's rainforests have disappeared.
4. Trees convert carbon dioxide into oxygen.
5. Rainforests maintain the Earth's temperature.

2 Read the passage to check.

About 50 per cent of rainforests are found in Central and South America. The rest are in central and West Africa, Southeast Asia and the Pacific Islands. The rainforests are home to half of the world's species of trees, birds and insects, but 50 per cent of our rainforests have disappeared in the last 50 years and hundreds of species of insect become extinct every week. If we destroy the rainforests, we destroy the world's lungs. This is because trees convert carbon dioxide into oxygen. Without the rainforests rainfall will decrease and temperatures will rise, increasing the greenhouse effect.

4 ACTION FILE

One way of protecting natural habitats is by conservation.

1 Draw a map of your country. Mark the nature reserves on it.

2 Choose a nature reserve near you.
- What type of reserve is it? (mountains, lake, etc.)
- What is the weather like in the winter and the summer?
- Which animals live in it?

3 Make a poster with the information.

117

The Guardians
INVESTIGATION FILE 4

1 WORD SEARCH

Match each word to its sound and translation.

a expense (n)	h /ʃɔːt tɜːm/	o a corto plazo
b famine (n)	i /krɒp/	p tierra
c hunger (n)	j /lænd/	q gastos
d short-term (adj)	k /ˈfæmɪn/	r cultivos
e land (n)	l /ɪkspens/	s cultivar
f grow (v)	m /ˈhʌŋgə/	t hambre
g crop (n)	n /grəʊ/	

2 EXPENSES

1 Match the words to the pictures.

food   heating   drink   clothes
transport   entertainment

2 Work in pairs.

1 Make a list of five items your family buys in a normal week.

2 Which is the most/least essential item?

3 RICH AND POOR

1 Read these questions.

1 What do people in rich countries do when there is famine in developing countries?

2 What is the problem with this kind of help?

3 What is most of the best land in developing countries used for?

4 Why is clean water important?

2 Read the passage and answer the questions.

Over half of the world's population lives in poverty. Millions of people die of hunger every year. In the last twenty years there have been serious famines in Ethiopia, Somalia and the Sudan. Rich countries send food, money and medicine, but help like this is only short-term. Developing countries need long-term aid which helps them to help themselves.

Three important problems for these countries are:

FOOD

Most of the best land is used to grow crops such as coffee and tobacco to sell to rich countries. Land for growing food to feed local people is usually of poor quality.

WATER

Over 2 billion people in these countries do not have access to clean water. Contaminated water is the major cause of the world's diseases which kill thousands of people a day.

MEDICAL SERVICES

Local medical and healthcare services do not exist in many parts of developing countries. There are few hospitals or qualified doctors and almost no medicines.

4 ACTION FILE

1 Complete the letter.

Oxfam
274 Branbury Road
London
ENGLAND

Dear Sir/Madam,
   I am writing for information about the problems facing developing countries.
   My name is 1_____ and I am from 2_____. I am 3_____ years old and go to 4_____ school.
   Please send the information to 5_____.
   Yours faithfully,
   6_____

2 Find out the address of an educational organisation which provides details of the problems facing developing countries.

3 Write to the organisation you chose and ask for some information about developing countries.

4 Make a poster with the information you receive.

118

1 WORD SEARCH

Match each word to its sound and translation.

a fossil fuel (n)   f /lɑːst/   k potencia
b last (v)   g /sɔːs/   l fuente
c power (n)   h /dæm/   m durar
d source (n)   i /ˈfɒsəl fjʊəl/   n combustible fósil
e dam (n)   j /ˈpaʊə/   o pantano

2 ENERGY

1 Are these statements true or false?
1 Coal, gas and oil are all fossil fuels.
2 The average person in the USA uses twice as much fuel as a European and a thousand times as much as a person from Somalia.
3 Coal reserves will last more than 500 years.
4 Man can manufacture new fossil fuels.
5 There are not many problems with nuclear power.
6 Nuclear power is more expensive than power from fossil fuels.
7 Nuclear power pollutes the atmosphere.
8 Nuclear waste is not active for very long.

2 Listen to check.

3 Write down any other information you hear.

3 ALTERNATIVE ENERGY

1 Are any sources of alternative energy mentioned in the text?

There are several important sources of alternative energy. Over 20 per cent of the world's electricity comes from dams and rivers. In parts of the USA wind farms generate 15 per cent of the electricity. In countries such as Hungary, Japan, Iceland and New Zealand, geothermal power produces a large proportion of energy. But the greatest potential source of energy is, of course, the sun. For years people have been developing solar power systems which convert sunlight into energy for domestic and industrial use. In fact many houses in North America and Scandinavia make all the energy they need from solar panels. This natural energy is the hope for the future. At the moment alternative sources of energy are expensive, but they will become cheaper. We should continue to research alternative sources of energy, so that we can protect our environment.

2 Are these statements true or false?
1 Dams and rivers provide 50 per cent of the world's energy.
2 Wind power is used in parts of the USA.
3 Geothermal power is important in Iceland.
4 Solar energy cannot be used in Scandinavian countries because of the climate.
5 Alternative energy is cheaper than other forms of energy.
6 Alternative energy is not harmful to the environment.

4 ACTION FILE

Turn off electrical appliances if you are not using them.

1 Do people use any forms of alternative energy in your country?

2 Draw a map of your country and label the places where people use alternative energy.

3 Invent a slogan which promotes the use of alternative energy. Make a poster explaining the importance of using alternative energy.

RICH & POOR

WASTE

119

The Guardians
INVESTIGATION FILE 6

1 WORD SEARCH

Match each word to its sound and translation.

a waste (n)   e /rɪ'zɔːs/   i recursos
b rubbish (n)   f /seɪv/   j salvar/ahorrar
c resource (n)   g /weɪst/   k basura
d save (v)   h /'rʌbɪʃ/   l residuos

2 WASTE

1 Match the words to the objects in the picture.

1 food waste   2 paper and card   3 glass
4 clothing   5 metal   6 plastic

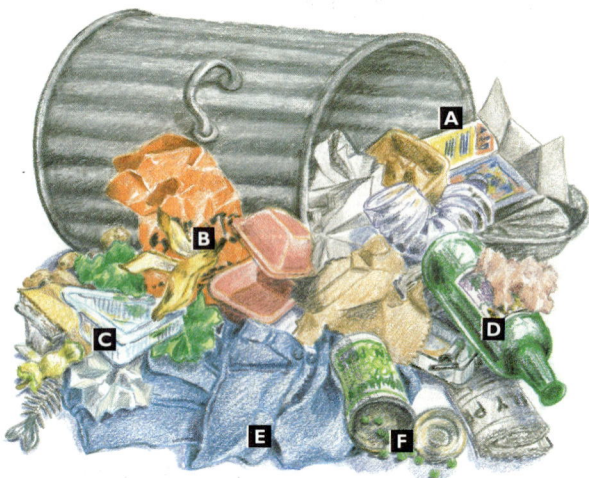

2 Use the information in the text to complete the bar graph.

We throw away millions of tonnes of rubbish every year. This rubbish contains a variety of material which we can recycle. If you emptied the contents of a typical domestic rubbish bin you would find that about a third was paper and card, especially from food packaging. About a quarter of the contents would be food waste, a tenth would be plastic and the rest equal parts of glass, cloth and metal.

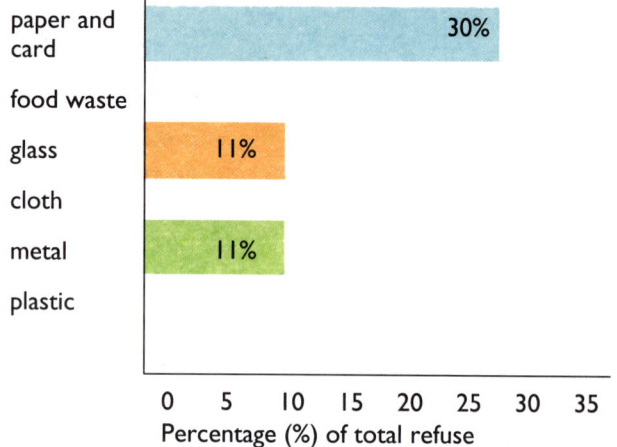

paper and card — 30%
food waste
glass — 11%
cloth
metal — 11%
plastic

Percentage (%) of total refuse

3 RECYCLING

What are the advantages of recycling waste? Read the text and make a list.

Many of the things we throw away can be recycled. Recycling can reduce pollution from certain products such as car oil and batteries. It can also prolong the life of limited reserves of other natural resources such as wood. It often saves energy too. For example, using recycled glass, rather than making new glass, saves energy so it is cheaper. Recycling also gives jobs to hundreds of people by creating new industries. So before you throw something away next time, stop and think!

4 ACTION FILE

Try to save paper and use bottles more than once.

1 Where are these places in your town? Mark them on a map.

a a place to leave used batteries
b a paper recycling plant
c a bottle bank

2 Use the map in a poster. Invent a slogan which promotes recycling waste.
Example:
Reuse supermarket carrier bags.

WASTE

120

FAST FORWARD

FF 1

Write the questions the shop assistant asks Mike.

FF 2

Write four questions the interviewer asks Simon.

FF 3

Are these sentences true or false?
1 She watches television in the morning.
2 She has a personal stereo.
3 Her favourite band is NKOTB.
4 She listens to music on her stereo before she does her homework.
5 Her friends like the same music.

FF 4

Look at the songs in the top ten list. Choose three and write your opinion about each one.
Example:
Madonna Holiday - *I think it's brilliant.*

FF 5

Write two sentences to describe what is happening in the first scene.

FF 6

1 Which words do you hear in the description?
tall short curly straight thin dark round muscular blond

2 Write the sentences.

FF 7

Write a list of mistakes the presenter makes.

FF 8

Write the contestant's incorrect answers.

FF 9

Listen and complete.
1 I'm ___ ___ a pair of trainers.
2 Have you got ___ ___?
3 ___ ___ these?
4 ___ ___ are they?
5 ___ ___ ___ for a drink?

FF 10

Write a list of brand names and products you hear.

FF 11

Write three words the fan uses to describe Kevin Costner.

FF 12

Write four things the teenagers say about Kylie Minogue.

FF 13

Write answers to these questions.
1 What is Mike doing on Friday?
2 Where is Susan going?
3 What does Dave think about Matt?

FF 14

1 Unjumble these expressions.
1 then time another
2 a hold minute on
3 love I'd to
4 me let think

2 What does each expression mean?

FF 15

Use the prompts to write out Dr Rufus' sentences.
1 antidote
2 full moon
3 dogs
4 garlic
5 go out alone

FF 16

Write a note for your friend explaining what he/she should or should not do to take care of your python while you are on holiday.

FF 17

1 Complete Anne's questions.
1 ___ ___ ___ school yet?
2 ___ ___ ___ a sports club yet?
3 ___ ___ ___ there since then?

2 Has Kate done these things?

FF 18

Answer these questions.
1 How long has the first caller had her puppy?
2 When did the second caller leave school?
3 What two suggestions does Jean have for the third caller?
4 What is the last caller going to do with the money he won?

FF 19

Write down four items of vocabulary you think are useful from the dialogue. Write the meanings of the words. Read the dialogue again to check.

FF 20

Write two sentences about what Richard has to and doesn't have to do at home.

FF 21

Make a list of all the things the cyclist did wrong.

FF 22

Look at the graph. Does Daniel have a good lifestyle? Why/Why not?

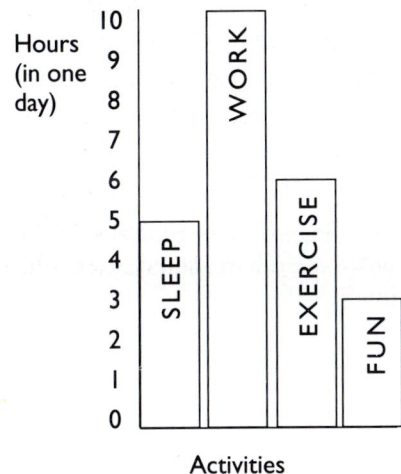

● FF 23

Write three answers Mike gives to the policeman.

● FF 24

Write five questions about the text with these words.
1 What
2 How many
3 When
4 Why
5 Where

● FF 25

Complete these sentences with the correct form of the verbs in brackets.
1 Carol ___ (start) to swim towards the island.
2 She ___ (cry) when she ___ (see) a boat.
3 The boat ___ (come) towards her.
4 The black shape ___ (follow) the boat.
5 Carol ___ (swim) faster and faster.
6 The island ___ (get) closer.
7 She ___ (stand up) and ___ (run) out of the water.

● FF 26

For each book write two things that the person on the radio says that are different from the reviews in your book.

● FF 27

Answer these questions.
1 Is Mike going to tell the police?
2 Is Mike going to go home with his dad?
3 Will Mike try to work harder?
4 Will Mike pass all his exams?

● FF 28

Choose two expressions and write your own sentence for each one.

● FF 29

Correct the information in these sentences.
1 Joan's legs started to hurt.
2 Suddenly, her hands touched something solid.
3 It was light in the tunnel.
4 Joan turned on her torch.
5 She was standing at the entrance to a secret room.

● FF 30

You will hear one sentence that does not appear in the text. Listen and write the sentence.

● FF 31

1 Listen to the dialogue. How many sentences include the second conditional?

2 Write one of them.

● FF 32

Write two of Rick's replies.

● FF 33

Susan's mum visits her in hospital and asks her four questions. Write the questions.

● FF 34

Write the three questions Susan asks her mother.

● FF 35

Copy and complete these sentences from the dialogue.
1 Well, the 24 is ___ of course, but then it's not ___ ___ ___ the 28.
2 The 24 has got a ___ ___ ___, but it isn't ___ ___.
3 Well, the 28 is one of ___ ___ ___ computers on the market.
4 The 24 isn't ___ ___ ___ the 28.
5 The 28 has got a ___ keyboard too.

● FF 36

Write three points about telephones, one about typewriters and one about computers.

● FF 37

Copy and complete these sentences.
1 They ___ ___ get into the spaceship.
2 ___ ___ ___ wear a spacesuit.
3 ___ ___ ___ visit their houses.
4 ___ ___ ___ eat strange food.
5 ___ ___ ___ pilot the spaceship.

● FF 38

You are 2B B2's master. He is looking after your house. Write four sentences telling him what to do.
Example:
I want you to feed the cat.

● FF 39

Listen to the dialogue. Copy and complete these sentences.
1 ___ was the place ___ ?
2 What about the people? What ___ ___ like?
3 What was ___ ___ ___ ?

● FF 40

For Sumatra, Java and Bali, name one place the people on the tour will visit.

● FF 41

Write a short dialogue between Mike and Susan.

● FF 42

What does Susan say about the following:
1 her visit to Mike
2 her accident
3 her mum's reaction

GRAMMAR REFERENCE

UNIT 1

Present simple (1): *be*

Form

Affirmative		Negative		Interrogative	
I	am (I'm)	I	am not (I'm not)	am	I ?
you	are (you're)	you	are not (aren't)	are	you?
he		he			he?
she	is (he's) (she's) (it's)	she	is not (isn't)	is	she?
it		it			it?
we		we			we?
you	are (we're) (you're) (they're)	you	are not (aren't)	are	you?
they		they			they?

Use

1 With adjectives.
Example: *He is gorgeous.*
2 With nouns.
Example: *They are singers.*
3 With prepositions.
Example: *We are from Italy.*

Note: Contractions are normally used when writing informally and when speaking.

Present simple (2): regular verbs

Form

Affirmative		Negative		Interrogative	
I	like	I			I	like?
you		you	do not (don't) like	do	you	
he		he			he	
she	likes	she	does not (doesn't) like	does	she	like?
it		it			it	
we		we			we	
you	like	you	do not (don't) like	do	you	like?
they		they			they	

Note 1: Negatives and questions are formed with *do*.
Note 2: For information about spelling for the 3rd person singular of the present simple, see Unit 2.
Note 3: *Like* can be followed by a noun or a verb. When it is followed by a verb, the verb is in the gerund.
Example: *I like comics. I like reading comics.*

Short answers

For information about short answers, see Unit 6.

UNIT 2

Adverbs (1): adverbs of frequency

Form

1 Adverbs of frequency usually go before the main verb.
Example: *I **always listen** to music in the morning.*
2 When the main verb is *be*, the adverb of frequency comes after it.
Example: *Madonna's concerts **are usually** fantastic.*
For information about other types of adverbs, see Unit 15.

Prepositions of time

Use

1 *At* is used for the time of day.
Example: *He goes to bed **at** 10.30.*
2 *In* is used for part of the day.
Example: *He studies **in** the afternoon.*
3 *On* is used for the days of the week.
Example: *He practises **on** Fridays.*
4 *During* is used for a period of time.
Example: *He goes to school **during** the week.*

Note: *At* is also used with *night* and *the weekend*.
For information about prepositions of place, see Unit 12.

Present simple

Spelling (3rd person)

1 For most verbs, add *-s*.
Example: *listen - listen**s***
2 For verbs that end in a consonant plus *-y*, change the *-y* to *-i* and add *-es*.
Example: *stud**y** - stud**ies***
3 For verbs ending in *-o*, add *-es*.
Example: *go - go**es***
4 For verbs ending in *-ch, -s, -sh, -x*, add *-es*.
Example: *watch - wat**ches**, wash - wa**shes***

Use

1 To talk about routines.
Example: *Graham practises with the band on Fridays.*
2 To talk about situations in the present which stay the same for a long time.
Example: *Graham lives in Manchester.*
For the use of the present simple in first conditional sentences, see Unit 8.

UNIT 3

Present continuous

Form
be + verb + *-ing* (present participle)

Spelling (present participle)

1 For most verbs, add *-ing* to the infinitive without *to*.
Example: *go - go**ing**, listen - listen**ing***
2 For verbs that end in *-e*, drop the *-e* and add *-ing*.
Example: *celebrate - celebrat**ing**, smile - smil**ing***
3 For verbs that end in *-y*, keep the *-y* and add *-ing*.
Example: *study - study**ing**, fly - fly**ing***
4 For verbs that end in a vowel and a consonant, double the consonant and add *-ing*.
Example: *sit - sit**ting**, stop - stop**ping***

Use

1 To talk about an action or situation which is taking place now and which has not yet finished.
Example: *Lola is going into a travel agent's.*
2 Compare the use of the present continuous and the present simple in these sentences.
Magnut is a private detective. He follows people.
(Present simple. This is routine for Magnut.)
Magnut is following Lola now.
(Present continuous. This is what Magnut is doing at the moment.)
For information about the future use of the present continuous, see Unit 7.

Have got

Form

Affirmative			Negative		Interrogative		
I you	have	(I've) (you've)	got	I you	have not (haven't) got	have	I you	got?
he she it	has	(he's) (she's) (it's)	got	he she it	has not (hasn't) got	has	he she it	got?
we you they	have	(we've) (you've) (they've)	got	we you they	have not (haven't) got	have	we you they	got?

Use

1 To talk about possessions.
Example: *Have you got a leather jacket?*
2 To talk about appearance.
Example: *She has got long hair and blue eyes.*

Note 1: *Have got* is used in spoken and informal written English. *Have* is preferred in formal written English. *Have* forms questions and negatives with *do*.
Example: *They do not have enough money to get to London.*
Note 2: *Got* is not repeated in short answers.
Example: *Has she got blue eyes? - No, she hasn't.*

UNIT 4

Simple past (1): *be*

Form

Affirmative		Negative			Interrogative	
I you	was were	I you	was not (wasn't) were not (weren't)		was were	I? you?
he she it	was	he she it	was not (wasn't)		was	he? she? it?
we you they	were	we you they	were not (weren't)		were	we? you? they?

Simple past (2): regular verbs

Form

Affirmative		Negative		Interrogative		
I you	played	I you	did not (didn't) play	did	I you	play?
he she it	played	he she it	did not (didn't) play	did	he she it	play?
we you they	played	we you they	did not (didn't) play	did	we you they	play?

Spelling

1 For most verbs, add -ed to the infinitive without *to*.
Example: *watch - watch**ed**, start - start**ed***
2 For verbs that end in -e, add -d.
Example: *compete - compet**ed**, introduce - introduc**ed***
3 For verbs that end in a consonant plus -y, drop the -y and add -ied.
Example: *study - stud**ied**, marry - marr**ied***

4 For verbs that end in a vowel and a consonant, double the consonant and add -ed.
Example: *travel - trave**lled**, stop - sto**pped***

Use

To talk about a completed action or state at a particular time in the past.
Example: *The Olympic Games started in Greece.*

Simple past (3): irregular verbs

Form

Except for *be*, all irregular verbs have an irregular form in the affirmative only. Questions and negatives are formed with *did*, in the same way as regular verbs.
Example: ***Did** John **win**? No, John **did not win**. Sheila **won**.*

UNIT 5

Comparatives and superlatives

Form

1 One-syllable adjectives

	comparative	superlative
most one-syllable adjectives cheap, long	*cheaper* *longer*	**the** *cheapest* **the** *longest*
adjectives ending with -e late, fine	*later* *finer*	**the** *latest* **the** *finest*
adjectives ending with a vowel and a consonant big, hot	*bigger* *hotter*	**the** *biggest* **the** *hottest*

2 Two syllable adjectives

	comparative	superlative
most two-syllable adjectives famous, useful	**more** *famous* **more** *useful*	**the most** *famous* **the most** *useful*
adjectives ending with -y friendly, heavy	*heavier* *friendlier*	**the** *heaviest* **the** *friendliest*

3 Longer adjectives

adjective	comparative	superlative
popular expensive	**more** *popular* **more** *expensive*	**the most** *popular* **the most** *expensive*

4 Irregular adjectives

adjective	comparative	superlative
good bad	*better* *worse*	*best* *worst*

Unit 6

Short answers

Form

Short answers are formed with *yes* or *no*, followed by a pronoun and an auxiliary verb (e.g. *be, do* and *have*) or a modal verb (e.g. *can*).
Is Gloria Estefan touring Europe at the moment? *Yes, she is.*
Do you think Kevin Costner is handsome? *No, I don't.*
Has Sinead O'Connor got a Rolls Royce? *No, she hasn't.*
Can your friends come to the cinema? *Yes, they can.*

Unit 7

The future (1): future arrangements

1 The present continuous indicates future arrangements that are already planned.
Example: *Matt is taking me to the cinema.*
2 It is usually clear from the context whether the present continuous has present or future meaning. Time expressions make this clearer.
Example: *What are you doing next weekend?*
For more information on the future, see Unit 10.

Can

Form

Can is a modal verb. Modal verbs do not change their form in the present (they do not take *-s* in the 3rd person singular) and they do not form questions and negatives with *do*. They are followed by an infinitive without *to*.

Note: Contracted form in the negative. *cannot - can't*

Use

1 To ask for, give or refuse permission.
Example: *Can I go to Jo's house, Mum? - No, you can't.*
2 To express ability.
Example: *Jim can swim, but he cannot play the guitar.*
Can refers to both physical ability (swimming) and to a skill (playing the guitar).
For information on other modal verbs, see Unit 8 (*should*), Unit 10 (*will*) and Unit 14 (*might*).

Unit 8

First conditional

Form

Affirmative
*If Jenny **sees** an elephant, she **will (she'll) take** a photo.*
Negative
*She **will not (won't) climb** a tree if she **does not feel** afraid.*
Interrogative
*What **will** she **do** if a lion **attacks** her?*
1 There are two parts to a first conditional sentence: the possibility (*if*-clause) and the result (main clause).
2 The verb describing the possibility is in the present and the verb describing the result is with *will*.
3 The meaning of the sentence does not change if the order of the clauses is reversed.
Example: *If she sees an elephant, she will take a photo.*
   or *She will take a photo if she sees an elephant.*

Use

To talk about something that is possible in the future. The event in the *if*-clause may happen (it is possible), or it may not. The main clause states the result of the event in the *if*-clause.
For information on the second conditional, see Unit 16.

Should

Form

Should is a modal verb. It does not change its form in the present (it does not take *-s* in the 3rd person singular) and it does not form questions and negatives with *do*. It is followed by an infinitive without *to*.

Note: Contracted form in the negative. *should not - shouldn't*

Use

To advise someone to do something.
Example: *If a dog bites you, you should go to the doctor.*
For more information on modal verbs, see Unit 7 (*can*), Unit 10 (*will*) and Unit 14 (*might*).

Unit 9

Present perfect simple

Form
have + past participle

1 The present perfect simple is formed with *have/has* and the past participle of the verb.
2 The past participle of regular verbs has the same form as the simple past.
Example: *play - played - played*

Use

1 To talk about general past experience when something happened at an unspecified time in the past. The present perfect simple is often used with *ever* or *never*.
Example: *Have you heard the new Prince album?*
      I have been to Paris, but I have not been to Rome.
*Has she **ever** been to the club? - I have **never** seen her there.*
2 To talk about a recent past experience that has a result in the present.
Example: *Peter has missed the bus and now he is standing in the rain.*
Here the present perfect simple is often used with *just*.
Example: *I have **just** won the lottery! Let's celebrate!*
3 The simple past is used to refer to a specific time in the past.
Example: *Have you ever been to the United States? - Yes, I have.*
      (Indefinite time - present perfect.)
      I went there last year. (Specific time - simple past.)
For information on the present perfect continuous, see Unit 17.

Unit 10

The future (2): future intentions

There are two main ways to express future intention in English: with *going to* and with *will*.

Form
1 *going to*
be + *going to* + infinitive

2 *will*
Will is a modal verb. It does not change its form in the present (it does not take *-s* in the 3rd person singular) and it does not form questions and negatives with *do*. It is followed by an infinitive without *to*.

Note: Contracted form in the negative. *will not - won't*

Use

Going to
To talk about something we intend to do in the future. *Going to* indicates that the future event was planned before the moment of speaking.
Example: *We are going to see Cats tomorrow.* (We have the tickets.)

Will
To express a sudden decision that the speaker makes at the moment of speaking. The speaker usually makes the decision in response to something that happens at that moment or something another person says.
Example: *I'm having a party. - I'll bring a cake if you like.*
For information about future arrangements, see Unit 7.

Obligation (1): *have to*

Form
have to + infinitive without *to*

Use

1 To express obligation. Usually the obligation is external (it comes from other people, not the speaker).
Example: *You have to be in class at nine.* (It is a rule of the school.)
I have to be in bed before ten. (My parents require it.)
2 *Do not have to* expresses lack of obligation. It is used to talk about something that we can do if we want, but which is not obligatory.
Example: *You do not have to walk to school. There is a bus.*
For more information about obligation, see Unit 19.

UNIT 11

Countable and uncountable nouns

1 Countable nouns refer to people or things that can be counted. They have a plural form.
Example: *banana - bananas, potato - potatoes*
2 Countable nouns take either a singular or a plural verb, depending on their meaning.
Example: *I cannot eat this banana. It is still green.*
    These bananas are enormous.
3 Uncountable nouns refer to things that cannot be counted. They do not have a plural form.
Example: *water, rice, bread*
4 Uncountable nouns only take a singular verb.
Example: *This rice is delicious.*
5 To specify the quantities of uncountable nouns, words such as *litre*, *kilo* and *bottle* are used.
Example: *a litre of water, a kilo of rice*

Quantifiers

1 Some quantifiers can be used with both countable and uncountable nouns.
Example: *a lot of, lots of, plenty of, not enough*
2 Other quantifiers can only be used with either countable or uncountable nouns.
Example:
countable nouns: *many, how many, too many, a few*
uncountable nouns: *much, how much, too much, a little*

How much? or *How many?*

How much is used with uncountable nouns. *How many* is used with countable nouns in the plural.
Example: *How much water is there in the bottle?*
    How many apples are there in your bag?

Much/many
These expressions are normally used in negative and interrogative sentences.
Example: *We have not got much money.*
    There are not many oranges on the table.
    Is there much milk in the bottle?
    Are there many potatoes in the cupboard?

A lot of/lots of/plenty of
These expressions are normally used in affirmative sentences with both countable and uncountable nouns. They are similar in meaning.
Example: *You use a lot of energy on a mountain bike.*
    Eat lots of raisins and drink plenty of water.

A little/a few
These expressions are normally used in affirmative sentences. *A little* is used with uncountable nouns and *a few* with countable nouns.
Example: *If you get very tired, drink a little water and eat a few nuts.*

Too much/too many/not enough
1 *Too much/many* means 'an excess of'.
Example: *Too much chocolate is bad for you.*
    She smokes too many cigarettes.
2 *Not enough* means 'not sufficient'. It can be used with both countable and uncountable nouns.
Example: *There is not enough food for everybody.*
    There are not enough chairs.

Too + adjective
With an adjective, *too* has the idea of excess.
Example: *The water here is too dirty to drink.*

UNIT 12

Prepositions of place
The following prepositions are used to describe the position of things in relation to one another.

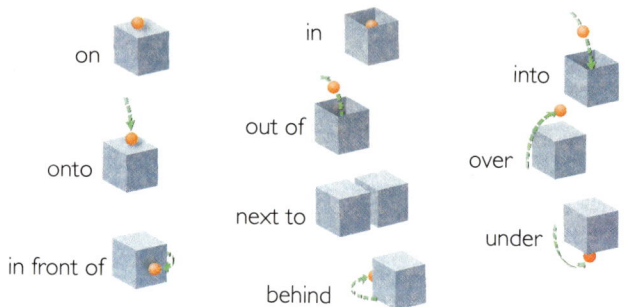

For information on prepositions of time, see Unit 2.

Question words (2)
How old is your teacher?
How often do you go to the cinema?
How many brothers and sisters have you got?
How much do you spend on CDs each month?
Why are you learning English?
Where do you usually go on holiday?
What sports do you play?
Who is your favourite sports personality?
When did you start studying English?

UNIT 13

Past continuous

Form
was/were + verb + *-ing* (present participle)
For information on spelling rules for the present participle, see Unit 3.

Use

1 To talk about an activity that was in progress at or around a point of time in the past.
Example: *I was watching television at eight o'clock last night.*
2 The past continuous is used with the simple past to indicate a state or activity in the past which was interrupted by an event.
Example: *Carol was swimming when she saw the black shape.*

Relative pronouns: *who, which* and *that*

Use

To give information about people or things.
1 *Who* is used for people.
Example: *I like books with **heroes who** are sensitive.*
2 *Which* is used for things.
Example: *I hate **stories which** have sad endings.*
3 *That* is used for people and things.
Example: *I read **the book that** Jonathan gave me. It is about **a girl that** finds a magic ring.*

Unit 14

Might

Form

Might is a modal verb. It does not change its form in the present (it does not take -s in the 3rd person singular) and it does not form questions and negatives with *do*. It is followed by an infinitive without *to*.
Note: Contracted form in the negative. *might not - mightn't*

Use

1 To talk about a future event if it is not certain that the event will happen. Example: *I might tell the police. I'm not sure.*
2 *Might* can be used instead of *will* in first conditional sentences when we are not sure that the event in the result (main clause) will happen.
Example: *If I go to the beach next summer, I might learn to surf or I might take tennis lessons.*
For information on other modal verbs, see Unit 7 (*can*), Unit 8 (*should*) and Unit 10 (*will*).

Unit 15

Adverbs (2)

Form

1 To form adverbs, add -ly to the adjective.
Example: *quick - quick**ly**, loud - loud**ly***
2 For adjectives that end in -y, change the -y to -i and add -ly.
Example: *happy - happ**ily***
3 Some adverbs have the same form as the adjective.
Example: *fast - fast, hard - hard*

Use

Adverbs describe the action expressed by the verb.
Example: *She **jumped** inside **quickly**.*
For information on adverbs of frequency, see Unit 2.

Purpose

Use

1 To explain the reason for doing something. The form is: verb + *to* + verb.
Example: *She **pushed** the rock **to see** if it moved.*
2 To explain what something is used for. The form is: noun + *for* + verb + -ing.
Example: *a saw for cutting wood*

Unit 16

Second conditional

Form
Affirmative
*If I **saw** £5 in the street, I **would (I'd) pick** it **up**.*
Negative
*If he **saw** £5 in the street, he **would not (wouldn't) pick** it **up**.*
Interrogative
*What **would** you **do** if you saw £5 in the street?*
1 There are two parts to a second conditional sentence: an improbable condition (*if*-clause) and an improbable result (main clause).
2 The verb in the *if*-clause is in the simple past and the verb in the main clause is with *would*.
3 If the verb in the *if*-clause is *be*, *were* is used for the 1st person.
Example: *If **I were** you, I would go.*
4 The meaning of the sentence does not change if the order of the clauses is reversed.
Example: *If I forgot to do my homework, I would tell the teacher. I would tell the teacher if I forgot to do my homework.*

Use

To talk about improbable/imaginary events in the future.
For information on the first conditional, see Unit 8.

Giving advice

Form

1 *What about* + verb + *-ing*
Example: *What about going to the cinema?*
2 *Why* + *do/does not* + verb
Example: *Why doesn't she talk to her teacher?*
3 Second conditional (1st person)
Example: *If I were you, I would tell the police.*
4 *Should*
Example: *You should see a doctor.*

Unit 17

Present perfect continuous

Form

have been + verb + *-ing* (present participle)

Use

1 To talk about activities or situations that started in the past and continue to the present. The continuous form is used to emphasise the length of time of the activity or the situation.
Example: *I have been running for three hours.* (I am really tired.)
We have been waiting for over two hours. (That is a long time.)
2 Some verbs are not normally used in the continuous form. These verbs describe states, rather than activities.
Here are some state verbs: *know, be, have, see, hear, like, hate, love.*
Example: *I **have known** my best friend for four years.*

How long? For/since

Use

1 *How long?*
To find out the length of time of an activity or situation, use *How long?* in the question.
Example: *How long have you been waiting?*

2 *For/since*
For refers to the length of the period of time.
Since refers to the start of the period of time.
Example: *I have been here **for two hours.***
*I have been here **since one o'clock**.*

Asking for and giving permission

Form
1 *Can/could*
Example: *Can I go out tonight?*
Could I borrow your skis for the weekend?
2 *Is it OK if* + present simple
Example: *Is it OK if I come home after midnight?*

Use
Could is more formal than *can* or *is it OK if*. It is used to ask permission for something which might be refused, or when we do not know the person we are asking very well.

UNIT 18

Comparison: *as...as*

Use
1 To compare things or people that are equal, use *as* + adjective + *as*.
Example: *The AX1 is **as big as** the AX2.*
2 To compare two things or people that are not equal, use *not as* + adjective + *as*.
Example: *The FAB is **not as expensive as** the PLC.*
For more information about comparison, see Unit 5.

Used to

Form
Affirmative
used to + infinitive without *to*
Negative
did not (didn't) use to + infinitive without *to*
Interrogative
did + subject + *use to* + infinitive without *to*

Use
1 To talk about activities repeated over a period of time in the past, but which are finished now.
Example: *I used to walk to school every day.* (I do not now)
2 To talk about states that were true in the past, but that are not true now.
Example: *I used to be good at tennis.* (I am not now)

UNIT 19

Make/let and *want*

Form
make and *let* + object + infinitive without *to*
want + object + infinitive
The object is usually the name of a person, or an object pronoun (*me, you, him, her, it, us, them*).

Use
1 *Make* is used to express external obligation.
Example: *My mother makes me help her at home.*
2 *Let* is used to express permission.
Example: *My grandparents let me eat anything I want.*
For more information on obligation, see Unit 10. For more information on permission, see Unit 7 and 17.

3 *Want* + object + infinitive is sometimes used to give instructions.
Example: *I want you to go to the supermarket and get some bread. Then I want you to come straight home. Don't stop at Daniel's house!*

UNIT 20

be like

Use
1 In questions *be like* is used to ask for someone's opinion about a place or thing.
Example: *What was Corfu like?* (What did you think of Corfu?)
What was the film like? (What did you think of the film?)
2 Another way to ask the same question is to use *how*.
Example: *How was Corfu?/How was the film?*
3 *Be like* is also used in questions to ask someone for their opinion of a person's character.
Example: *What is Vanessa like? - She is really nice. She has got a great sense of humour.*

Note 1: *How* is only used with people to ask about a person's health.
Example: *How is your mother? - She is fine, thanks.*
Note 2: The difference between *be like*, and the verb *like*.
Example: *What is Vanessa like? - She is really nice.*
What does Vanessa like? - She likes sport and music.

would like

Form
Would is a modal verb. It does not change its form in the present (it does not add *-s* in the 3rd person singular) and it does not form questions and negatives with *do*. It is followed by an infinitive without *to*.
Example: *Where would you like to go?*
Note: Contracted form in the negative. *would not - wouldn't*

Use
A common use of *would like* is to ask for information.
For the use of *would* in the second conditional, see Unit 16.

UNIT 21

Talking about the present
The tenses referring to the present in this book are:
Present simple (Unit 1 and 2)
Present continuous (Unit 3)
Present perfect simple (Unit 9)
Present perfect continuous (Unit 17)
The perfect tenses refer to the present in that the period of time they refer to includes the present, though it began in the past.

Talking about the past
The tenses referring to the past covered in this book are:
Simple past (Unit 4)
Past continuous (Unit 13)

Talking about the future
Aspects of the future covered in this book are:
Future arrangements using the present continuous (Unit 7)
Future intentions using *going to* and *will* (Unit 10)